Pocket
AMSTERDAM

TOP SIGHTS • LOCAL LIFE • MADE EASY

Karla Zimmerman

In This Book

QuickStart Guide

Your keys to understanding the city – we help you decide what to do and how to do it

Need to Know
Tips for a smooth trip

Neighbourhoods
What's where

Explore Amsterdam

The best things to see and do, neighbourhood by neighbourhood

Top Sights
Make the most of your visit

Local Life
The insider's city

The Best of Amsterdam

The city's highlights in handy lists to help you plan

Best Walks
See the city on foot

Amsterdam's Best...
The best experiences

Survival Guide

Tips and tricks for a seamless, hassle-free city experience

Getting Around
Travel like a local

Essential Information
Including where to stay

Our selection of the city's best places to eat, drink and experience:

◎ **Sights**

✖ **Eating**

🍷 **Drinking**

✪ **Entertainment**

🔒 **Shopping**

These symbols give you the vital information for each listing:

- ☏ Telephone Numbers
- ☺ Opening Hours
- P Parking
- ⊖ Nonsmoking
- @ Internet Access
- 📶 Wi-Fi Access
- 🥗 Vegetarian Selection
- 🍽 English-Language Menu
- 👪 Family-Friendly
- 🐾 Pet-Friendly
- 🚌 Bus
- ⛴ Ferry
- M Metro
- S Subway
- 🚊 Tram
- 🚆 Train

Find each listing quickly on maps for each neighbourhood:

Bar Hemingway

16 🍷 Map p233, B2

Legend has it that Hemi self, wielding a machine ...erate this timber-pan ...ered bar during ... showpiece is a ... en by Papa ar ... town. Dress ...s.com; Hôtel Rit ; ☺6.30pm-2a

6 ◎ Plac

Lonely Planet's Amsterdam

Lonely Planet Pocket Guides are designed to get you straight to the heart of the city.

Inside you'll find all the must-see sights, plus tips to make your visit to each one really memorable. We've split the city into easy-to-navigate neighbourhoods and provided clear maps so you'll find your way around with ease. Our expert authors have searched out the best of the city: walks, food, nightlife and shopping, to name a few. Because you want to explore, our 'Local Life' pages will take you to some of the most exciting areas to experience the real Amsterdam.

And of course you'll find all the practical tips you need for a smooth trip: itineraries for short visits, how to get around, and how much to tip the guy who serves you a drink at the end of a long day's exploration.

It's your guarantee of a really great experience.

Our Promise

You can trust our travel information because Lonely Planet authors visit the places we write about, each and every edition. We never accept freebies for positive coverage, so you can rely on us to tell it like it is.

QuickStart Guide 7

Explore Amsterdam 21

Worth a Trip:

The Best of Amsterdam 151

Amsterdam's Best Walks

Amsterdam's Best ...

Survival Guide 173

QuickStart Guide

Welcome to Amsterdam

Amsterdam works its fairy-tale magic in many ways: via the gabled, Golden Age buildings; glinting, boat-filled canals; and especially the cosy, centuries-old *bruin cafés* (traditional pubs), where candles burn low and beers froth high. Add in mega art museums and cool street markets, and it's easy to see why this atmospheric city is one of Europe's most popular getaways.

One of Amsterdam's many canals
JOHN WILKINSON / GETTY IMAGES ©

Amsterdam Top Sights

Van Gogh Museum (p86)

You'll wait in line outside and jostle with the crowds inside, but seeing those vivid brushstrokes of yellow sunflowers and purple-blue irises makes it all worthwhile.

Anne Frank Huis (p44)

Walking into the Secret Annexe, standing in Anne's melancholy bedroom and seeing the red-plaid diary itself is an undeniably powerful experience that draws a million visitors annually.

Rijksmuseum (p90)

The Netherlands' top treasure house bursts with Golden Age paintings, blue-and-white Delft pottery and gilded dollhouses. Rembrandt's humongous, gape-worthy *Night Watch* leads the pack.

Museum het Rembrandthuis (p126)

Step into the Dutch icon's inner sanctum and immerse yourself in his studio, where soft light streams in through the windows, and seashells, animal horns and other exotica weigh down the shelves.

Vondelpark (p94)

On sunny days it seems the whole city converges on this sprawling urban idyll. Joggers, picnickers, kissing couples, accordion players and frolicking children all throng the lawns, thickets and cafes.

Royal Palace (p24)

Enter the King's digs and ogle the tapestries, chandeliers, Italian marble and frescoed ceilings while getting a history lesson in Dutch royalty and politics.

Amsterdam Local Life
Local Life

Insider tips to help you find the real city

After seeing the tourist sights, seek out the offbeat music clubs, bohemian artist quarters, sweet patisseries and quirky local shops that make up the locals' Amsterdam. Count on brown *cafés* (traditional pubs) and canals making appearances.

Shopping the Jordaan & Western Canals (p46)

▸ Small, oddball shops
▸ Brown *cafés*

You probably didn't realise you needed antique eyeglasses or a handbound art book until now. But these surprises happen as you ramble the enchanted web of lanes. The other thing that happens: you'll get lost. No worries. Atmospheric *cafés* pop up to lend a guiding beverage.

Discovering Bohemian De Pijp (p106)

▸ Amsterdam's biggest market
▸ Hip restaurants and bars

De Pijp is like its own little village: people from all walks of life – workers, intellectuals, immigrants, prostitutes – mingle at the neighbourhood-spanning street market, then take the conversation to the arty eateries and jazzy little bars.

Strolling the Southern Canal Belt (p68)

▸ Golden Age mansions
▸ Swanky antique shops

Get a feel for the posh side of Amsterdam around the Southern Canals, one of the city's top addresses from the get-go. Seventeenth-century millionaires built double-wide homes here, and today's classy touches include the flower market, the antique quarter and some opulent theatres.

Café-Hopping in Nieuwmarkt & Plantage (p128)

▸ Flea market
▸ *Cafés* in historic buildings

Among the city's oldest and leafiest districts, Nieuwmarkt and the Plantage have an embarrassment of riches when it comes to places to relax and swill. No wonder locals flock here to hang out in between market browsing and gazing at contemporary art.

The Singel 404 cafe (p55), Jordaan & Western Canals area

Exploring Westerpark & Western Islands (p64)

Clogs at the Albert Cuypmarkt (p106), De Pijp

▶ Amsterdam School architecture
▶ Edgy cultural park

Amsterdam doesn't get much cooler than these two enclaves in the city's northwest corner. Get ready for drawbridge-strewn islands and a sprawling green space that melds bird-rich marshes with DJ-spinning *cafés* and jazz clubs.

Other great places to experience the city like a local:

De Hallen (p98)

De Twee Zwaantjes (p57)

Wil Graanstra Friteshuis (p54)

Oudemanhuis Book Market (p40)

Tokoman (p135)

Oosterpark (p122)

Rob Wigboldus Vishandel (p32)

Café Sarphaat (p114)

Utrechtsestraat (p79)

Lindengracht Market (p60)

Amsterdam Day Planner

Day One

Begin with the biggies: tram to the Museum Quarter to ogle the masterpieces at the **Van Gogh Museum** (p86) and **Rijksmuseum** (p90). They'll be crowded, so make sure you've prebooked tickets. Modern-art buffs might want to swap in the **Stedelijk Museum** (p97) for one of the others.

Spend the afternoon in the medieval City Centre. Have lunch at slow-food favourite **Gartine** (p30). Explore the secret courtyard and gardens at the **Begijnhof** (p28). Walk up the street to the **Dam** (p30), where the **Royal Palace** (p24) and **Nieuwe Kerk** (p29) huddle and provide a dose of Dutch history. Lean over and take your *jenever* (Dutch gin) like a local at **Wynand Fockink** (p34).

Do elegant Dutch for dinner at **Greetje** (p135), then venture into the Red Light District. A walk down Warmoesstraat or Oudezijds Achterburgwal provides an eye-popping line-up of fetish-gear shops, smoky coffeeshops and, of course, women in dayglo lingerie beckoning from crimson windows. Then settle in to a brown *café* (pub), such as **In 't Aepjen** (p35), **In de Olofspoort** (p36) or **'t Mandje** (p36).

Day Two

Browse the **Albert Cuypmarkt** (p106), Amsterdam's largest street bazaar, an international free-for-all of cheeses, fish, *stroopwafels* (syrup waffles) and bargain-priced clothing. Then submit to the **Heineken Experience** (p109) to get shaken up, heated up and 'bottled' like the beer you'll drink at the end of the brewery tour.

Have a burger at the **Butcher** (p111) for lunch. Make your way over to the Southern Canal Belt and stroll along the grand **Golden Bend** (p69). Visit **Museum Van Loon** (p72) for a peek into the opulent canal-house lifestyle, or see the lifestyle with a dose of kitty quirk at the **Kattenkabinet** (p69). Tour the glinting waterways with **Those Dam Boat Guys** (p171) or **Blue Boat Company** (p171).

For dinner, fork into organic dishes canal-side at **Buffet van Odette** (p75). Then it's time to par-tee at hyperactive, neon-lit Leidseplein. The clubs **Paradiso** (p80) and **Melkweg** (p80) host the coolest agendas. Otherwise the good-time bars and *cafés* around the square beckon, such as historic **Eijlders** (p78).

Short on time?
We've arranged Amsterdam's must-sees into these day-by-day itineraries to make sure you see the very best of the city in the time you have available.

Day Three

☼ Explore the Harbour and Eastern Islands' cutting-edge design. Stop in at **ARCAM** (p145) to arm yourself with architectural information, then head onward to the sea treasures at **Het Scheepvaartmuseum** (p144) and views from **NEMO** (p144) and the **Centrale Bibliotheek Amsterdam** (p144).

☼ Go west – as in Western Canals – and fork into sweet or savoury **Pancakes!** (p56) Immerse yourself in the surrounding **Negen Straatjes** (Nine Streets; p47), a tic-tac-toe board of oddball speciality shops. The **Anne Frank Huis** (p44) is also in the neighbourhood, and it's a must. The claustrophobic rooms, their windows still covered with blackout screens, give an all-too-real feel for Anne's life in hiding.

☽ Spend the evening in the Jordaan, the chummy district touted as the Amsterdam of yore. Eat in the old blacksmith's forge at **Balthazar's Keuken** (p52). Kitschy **Moeders** (p56) cooks up traditional Dutch dishes. Afterwards, hoist a glass on a canal-side terrace at **'t Smalle** (p56), join the drunken sing-along at **De Twee Zwaantjes** (p57), or quaff beers at heaps of other *gezellig* (cosy) haunts.

Day Four

☼ Take a spin through **Waterlooplein Flea Market** (p129). Doc Martens? Buddha statues? Electric saw? These goods and more fill the stalls. Rembrandt sure loved markets, if his nearby studio is any indication. **Museum het Rembrandthuis** (p126) gives a peek at the master's inner sanctum, including his curio-packed cabinet and paint-spattered easel. Neighbouring **Gassan Diamonds** (p132) gives the bling low-down via free tours.

☼ Munch delicious Surinamese sandwiches at **Tokoman** (p135). Mosey over to the Plantage to see the WWII resistance exhibits at the **Verzetsmuseum** (p132). Next it's time for an only-in-Amsterdam experience: drinking organic beer at the foot of an authentic windmill at **Brouwerij 't IJ** (p137). Snap your photos before knocking back too many glasses of the strong suds.

☽ You've been a sightseeing trouper, zipping through most of Amsterdam's neighbourhoods over the past four days. An evening spent plopped on the terrace at **De Ysbreeker** (p122), looking out over the bustling, houseboat-strewn Amstel River, is a well-deserved treat. Or take a seat on the rooftop at clubby **Canvas** (p122) and soak up the view.

Need to Know

For more information, see Survival Guide (p173)

Currency
Euro (€)

Language
Dutch and English

Visas
Generally not required for stays up to three months. Some nationalities require a Schengen visa.

Money
ATMs widely available. Credit cards accepted in most hotels but not all restaurants. Non-European credit cards are sometimes rejected.

Mobile Phones
Local SIM cards can be used in European and Australian phones. Standard North American GSM 1900 phones will not work.

Time
Central European Time (GMT/UTC plus one hour).

Plugs & Adaptors
Plugs have two round pins; electrical current is 220V. North American visitors will require an adaptor and a transformer.

Tipping
Leave 5% to 10% for a cafe snack (or round up to the next euro), 10% or so for a restaurant meal. Tip taxi drivers 5% to 10%.

❶ Before You Go

Your Daily Budget

Budget less than €100
- ▶ Dorm bed €25–€50
- ▶ Boom Chicago late-night-show ticket €14
- ▶ GVB transit day pass €7.50

Midrange €100–€250
- ▶ Double room €150
- ▶ Three-course dinner in casual eatery €35
- ▶ Concertgebouw ticket €40

Top end more than €250
- ▶ Four-star hotel double room €250
- ▶ Five-course dinner in top restaurant €60
- ▶ Private canal-boat rental for two hours €90

Useful Websites

- ▶ **Lonely Planet** (www.lonelyplanet.com/amsterdam) Destination information, hotel bookings, traveller forum and more.

- ▶ **I Amsterdam** (www.iamsterdam.com) City-run portal packed with sightseeing, accommodation and event info.

- ▶ **Dutch News** (www.dutchnews.nl) News tidbits and event listings.

Advance Planning

- ▶ **Six months before** Book your hotel, especially if you'll be visiting in summer.

- ▶ **Two months before** Check calendars for the Concertgebouw, Muziekgebouw aan 't IJ, Melkweg and Paradiso, and buy tickets for anything that appeals.

- ▶ **One week before** Buy tickets online to the Van Gogh Museum, Anne Frank Huis and Rijksmuseum. Book walking or cycling tours, and your must-eat restaurants.

② Arriving in Amsterdam

Most people flying to Amsterdam arrive at Schiphol International Airport (AMS; www.schiphol.nl), 18km southwest of the city centre. National and international trains arrive at Centraal Station (CS) in the city centre.

✈ From Schiphol Airport

Destination	Best Transport
City Centre, Jordaan, Western Canals	Train to Centraal Station
Nieuwmarkt, Plantage	Train to Centraal Station
De Pijp, Southern Canal Belt	Train to Centraal Station
Vondelpark, Old South, Leidseplein	Bus 197

🚋 From Centraal Station

Destination	Best Transport
City Centre & Red Light District	Tram 1, 2, 4, 5, 9, 16, 24
Jordaan & Western Canals	Tram 1, 2, 5, 13, 17
Southern Canal Belt	Tram 1, 2, 4, 5, 9
Vondelpark & Old South	Tram 1, 2, 5
De Pijp	Tram 16, 24

At the Airport/Train Station

Schiphol International Airport Has ATMs, currency exchanges, tourist information, car hire, train ticket sales, luggage storage, restaurants, shops and free wi-fi.

Centraal Station Has ATMs, currency exchanges, tourist information, restaurants, shops, luggage storage and train ticket sales.

③ Getting Around

Walking and cycling are the primary ways to travel around the small, densely packed city. GVB passes in chip-card form are the most convenient option for public transport. Buy them at visitor centres or from tram conductors. Always wave your card at the pink-logoed machine when entering and departing.

🏃 Walking

Central Amsterdam is compact and very easy to cover by foot.

🚲 Bicycle

Cycling is locals' main mode of getting around. Rental companies are all over town; bikes cost about €11 per day.

🚊 Tram

Trams are fast, frequent and ubiquitous, operating between 6am and 12.30am. A one-hour fare is €2.90, a day pass is €7.50.

🚌 Bus & Metro

The bus and metro systems primarily serve the outer districts; they're not much use in the city centre. Same fare as trams.

⛴ Ferry

Free ferries depart for northern Amsterdam from docks behind Centraal Station.

🚗 Taxi

Taxis are expensive and not very speedy given Amsterdam's maze of streets. Fares are €2.17 per kilometre; the meter starts at €2.95.

Amsterdam Neighbourhoods

City Centre (p22)

The busiest section of town for visitors, Amsterdam's medieval core mixes fairy-tale Golden Age buildings, brown *cafés* and the lurid Red Light District.

◉ Top Sights

Royal Palace (Koninklijk Paleis)

Jordaan & Western Canals (p42)

The Jordaan teems with cosy pubs and lanes ideal for getting lost. The Western Canals unfurl quirky boutiques and waterside *cafés*.

◉ Top Sights

Anne Frank Huis

Vondelpark & Old South (p84)

Vondelpark is a green lung with personality, adjacent to the genteel Old South, home to Amsterdam's grandest museums.

◉ Top Sights

Van Gogh Museum

Rijksmuseum

Vondelpark

De Pijp (p104)

Ethnic meets trendy in this recently gentrified neighbourhood, best sampled at the colourful Albert Cuypmarkt and multicultural eateries that surround it.

Anne Frank Huis ◉

◉ *Royal Palace (Koninklijk Paleis)*

Vondelpark ◉

Rijksmuseum ◉

Van Gogh Museum ◉

Worth a Trip
Local Life
Westerpark & Western Islands (p64)

Harbour & Eastern Islands (p140)
The harbour's hip, ever-changing skyline extends into the edgy Eastern Islands, adored by the design clique for its architectural experimentation.

Museum het Rembrandthuis

Nieuwmarkt & Plantage (p124)
See Rembrandt's studio and Amsterdam's Jewish heritage in Nieuwmarkt, and gardens and a beery windmill in the Plantage.

Top Sights
Museum het Rembrandthuis

Southern Canal Belt (p66)
By day, visit the city's less-heralded museums. By night, party at the clubs around Leidseplein and Rembrandtplein.

Oosterpark & Around (p116)
The Oost is one of the city's most culturally diverse neighbourhoods, with Moroccan and Turkish enclaves and some great bars and restaurants.

Explore
Amsterdam

Worth a Trip

An Amsterdam canal at sunrise
DENNIS VAN DE WATER / SHUTTERSTOCK ©

Explore

City Centre

Amsterdam's heart beats in its medieval core. The Royal Palace rises up on the main square, but the main thing to do is wander the twisting lanes past 17th-century pubs, hidden gardens and wee speciality shops. As for the infamous Red Light District, far from being a no-go area, it has some beautiful historic *cafés*, plus the stunning Oude Kerk.

The Sights in a Day

🔆 Fuel up with coffee and pastries at **Gartine** (p30). Nearby, look for the secret courtyard at the **Begijnhof** (p28). Pop into the **Amsterdam Museum** (p28) to learn local history, then see it in person at the **Dam** (p30), where the city was founded. The 15th-century **Nieuwe Kerk** (p29) and 17th-century **Royal Palace** (p24) also huddle here.

🔆 Grab a sandwich at **'Skek** (p33), and venture into the Red Light District. There's more here than you think. The 700-year-old **Oude Kerk** (p28) has a who's who of famous folks buried beneath its floor, while **Museum Ons' Lieve Heer op Solder** (p28) hides a relic-rich church behind its canalhouse façade. You can see titillating stuff too: walk down Warmoesstraat or Oudezijds Achterburgwal, past **Mr B** (p41) and **Casa Rosso** (p38).

🌙 Fork into *stamppot* and other Dutch specialities at **Haesje Claes** (p33). Belly up to the bar for a Dutch *jenever* (gin) at **Wynand Fockink** (p34) or **In de Olofspoort** (p36). Or sip at **Hoppe** (p35) on the Spui, a *café*-ringed plaza that is the city's intellectual hub.

👁 Top Sights
Royal Palace (p24)

♥ Best of Amsterdam

Eating
Gartine (p30)

Drinking & Nightlife
Wynand Fockink (p34)

Hoppe (p35)

In 't Aepjen (p35)

Café Belgique (p35)

Museums & Galleries
Amsterdam Museum (p28)

Museum Ons' Lieve Heer op Solder (p28)

Civic Guard Gallery (p29)

Getting There

🚊 **Tram** Most of Amsterdam's 15 tram lines go through the neighbourhood en route to Centraal Station. Busy ones include trams 4, 9, 16 and 24, which go by way of the Dam, and trams 1, 2 and 5, which go by the Spui.

⛴ **Boat** Free ferries run to Amsterdam-Noord, departing from the piers behind Centraal Station.

Top Sights
Royal Palace

Welcome to the King's house. If he's away, you're welcome to come in and wander around. Today's Royal Palace began life as a glorified town hall, and was completed in 1665. The architect, Jacob van Campen, spared no expense to display Amsterdam's wealth in a way that rivalled the grandest European buildings of the day. The result is opulence on a big scale.

Koninklijk Paleis

👁 Map p26, B5

📞 620 40 60

www.paleisamsterdam.nl

Dam Square

adult/child €10/free

🕙 10am-5pm

🚊 4/9/16/24 Dam

The Royal Palace on National Tulip Day

Don't Miss

The Tribunal

Start at the ground floor's Tribunal. This was the original court where magistrates meted out death sentences. The sinister sculptures of skulls and serpents underscore the chamber's severe purpose.

The Halls' Treasures

Most of the palace's rooms spread over the 1st floor, which is awash in chandeliers (51 shiners in total), damasks, gilded clocks and rich paintings by Ferdinand Bol and Jacob de Wit. The great *burgerzaal* (citizens' hall) that occupies the heart of the building was envisioned as a schematic of the world, with Amsterdam as its centre. Check out the maps inlaid in the floor; they show the eastern and western hemispheres, with a 1654 celestial map plopped in the middle.

King Louis' Gifts

In 1808 the building became the palace of King Louis, Napoleon Bonaparte's brother. In a classic slip-up in the new lingo, French-born Louis told his subjects here that he was the '*konijn* (rabbit) of Holland', whereas he meant *konink* (king). Napoleon dismissed him two years later. Louis left behind about 1000 pieces of Empire-style furniture and decorative artworks. As a result, the palace now holds one of the world's largest collections from the period.

Today's Palace

Officially King Willem-Alexander lives here and pays a symbolic rent, though he really resides in Den Haag. The palace is still used to entertain foreign heads of state and for other official business.

☑ Top Tips

▶ Pick up a free audio tour (available in multiple languages) at the desk after you enter. It greatly enhances a visit, as there isn't much signage.

▶ The palace often closes for state functions, especially during April, May, November and December. The website posts the schedule; check before heading out.

▶ E-tickets (with no surcharge), which provide fast-track entry, are available. The palace accepts them in both print and mobile formats.

▶ Queues typically are shorter late in the afternoon.

✗ Take a Break

Sample the famed Dutch herring on a fluffy white roll at Rob Wigboldus Vishandel (p32). Wash it down with the strong brews at Café Belgique (p35).

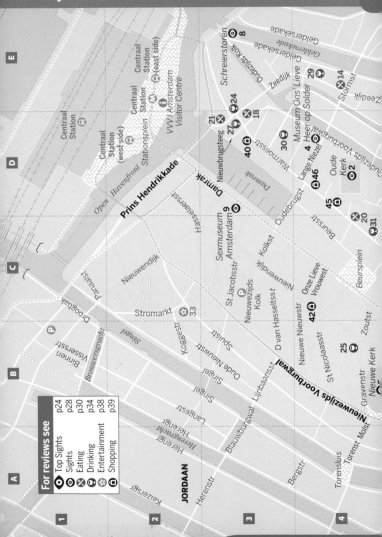

NIEUWMARKT

Koningsstr
Keizersstr
Dijkstr
Oude schans
Schans

Nieuwmarkt
St Antoniesbreestr

Nieuwmarkt
Nieuwe Hoogstr
Zandstr

Bloedstr

✕15
Koestr
Oude Hoogstr

34
10
Oudezijds Achterburgwal
Cannabis College

Kloveniersburgwal
Rusland
Slijkstr
Zwanenburgwal
Staalstr
Zwanenburgwal

Stopera

200 m
0.1 miles

N

Amstel

St Annenstr
Oudezijds Voorburgwal

✕32

CENTRUM
22
Pijlst
Damstr
Oudezijds Voorburgwal

Binnengasthuis
UvA
Nieuwe Doelenstr
Binnen Amstel

Warmoesstr

✕16
St Pietershalst
✕36

Nes
35
Grimburgwal

✕13
Oude Turfmarkt

41

Dam
7

Damrak

Kalverstr

Wijde Kapelst
Enge Kapelst

39

Rokin

Kalverstr
Muntplein

Royal Palace
(Koninklijk Paleis)

Jonge Roelenst
St Lucienst
Nieuwezijds Voorburgwal

Amsterdam Museum
Wilde Kapelst
Civic Guard Gallery

3
6
✕19
26

Taksteeg
11

✕12
Voetboogstr
28
Handboogstr
Heiligeweg
Singel

Magna Plaza

44

Gasthuismolenst
Paleisstr
Spuistr
Singel
Singel

Rosma-rijnst
43
✕17

Raamst

Begijnhof
1

38

23

Spui
Rokin
Rozenboomst

Valkenstr

Singel

Sights

Begijnhof
SQUARE

1 Map p26, A7

This enclosed former convent dates from the early 14th century. It's a surreal oasis of peace, with tiny houses and postage-stamp gardens around a well-kept courtyard. The Beguines were a Catholic order of unmarried or widowed women who cared for the elderly and lived a religious life without taking monastic vows. The last true Beguine died in 1971. (622 19 18; www.begijnhofamsterdam.nl; off Gedempte Begijnensloot; admission free; 9am-5pm; 1/2/5 Spui)

Oude Kerk
CHURCH

2 Map p26, D4

This is Amsterdam's oldest surviving building (from 1306). It's also an intriguing moral contradiction: a church surrounded by active Red Light District windows. Inside, check out the stunning Müller organ, the naughty 15th-century carvings on the choir stalls, and famous Amsterdammers' tombstones in the floor (including Rembrandt's wife, Saskia van Uylenburgh). The church often holds art exhibitions. You can also climb the tower on a guided tour. (Old Church; 625 82 84; www.oudekerk.nl; Oudekerksplein 23; adult/child €7.50/free; 10am-6pm Mon-Sat, 1-5:30pm Sun; 4/9/16/24 Dam)

Amsterdam Museum
MUSEUM

3 Map p26, B7

Amsterdam's history museum is a spiffy place to learn about what makes the city tick. Start with the multimedia DNA exhibit, which breaks down Amsterdam's 1000-year history into seven whiz-bang time periods. Afterward, plunge into the maze-like lower floors to see troves of religious artefacts, porcelains and paintings. Bonus points for finding Rembrandt's macabre *Anatomy Lesson of Dr Deijman*. The museum is a good choice during soggy weather, as there's rarely a queue. (523 18 22; www.amsterdammuseum.nl; Kalverstraat 92; adult/child €12/6; 10am-5pm; 1/2/5 Spui)

Museum Ons' Lieve Heer op Solder
MUSEUM

4 Map p26, D4

What looks like an ordinary canal house turns out to have an entire Catholic church stashed inside. Ons' Lieve Heer op Solder (Our Dear Lord in the Attic) was built in the mid-1600s in defiance of the Calvinists. Inside you'll see labyrinthine staircases, rich artworks, period decor and the soaring, two-storey church itself. The museum completed a multi-year restoration project in late 2015, so the interior now sparkles. (624 66 04; www.opsolder.nl; Oudezijds Voorburgwal 40; adult/child €9/4.50; 10am-5pm Mon-Sat, 1-5pm Sun; 4/9/16/24 Centraal Station)

Begijnhof

Nieuwe Kerk CHURCH

5 🎯 Map p26, B4

This 15th-century, late-Gothic basilica – a historic stage for Dutch coronations – is only 'new' in relation to the Oude Kerk. A few monumental items dominate the otherwise spartan interior – a magnificent carved oak chancel, a bronze choir screen, a massive organ and enormous stained-glass windows. The building is now used for exhibitions and organ concerts. Opening times and admission fees can vary, depending on what's going on. (New Church; ☎ 638 69 09; www.nieuwekerk. nl; Dam; admission €8-16; ⏰ 10am-5pm; 🚊 1/2/4/5/9/16/24 Dam)

Civic Guard Gallery GALLERY

6 🎯 Map p26, B7

This cool gallery is part of the Amsterdam Museum – consider it the free 'teaser' – and fills an alleyway next to the museum's entrance. It displays grand posed-group portraits, from medieval guards painted during the Dutch Golden Age (à la Rembrandt's *Night Watch*) to *Modern Civic Guards,* a rendering of Anne Frank, Alfred Heineken and a joint-smoking personification of Amsterdam. (Kalverstraat 92; admission free; ⏰ 10am-5pm; 🚊 1/2/5 Spui)

Dam SQUARE

7 👁 Map p26, B5

This square is the very spot where Amsterdam was founded around 1270. Today pigeons, tourists, buskers and the occasional Ferris-wheel-boasting fair take over the grounds. It's still a national gathering spot, and if there's a major speech or demonstration it's held here. (🚊4/9/16/24 Dam)

Schreierstoren HISTORIC BUILDING

8 👁 Map p26, E3

Built around 1480 as part of the city's defenses, this tower is where Henry Hudson set sail for the New World in 1609; a plaque outside marks the spot. It's called the 'wailing tower' in lore – where women waved farewell to sailors' ships – but the name actually comes from the word 'sharp' (for how the corner jutted into the bay). (www.schreierstoren.nl; Prins Hendrikkade 94-95; 🚊4/9/16/24 Centraal Station)

Sexmuseum Amsterdam MUSEUM

9 👁 Map p26, D3

The Sexmuseum is good for a giggle. You'll find replicas of pornographic Pompeian plates, erotic 14th-century Viennese bronzes, some of the world's earliest nude photographs, an automated farting flasher in a trench coat, and a music box that plays 'Edelweiss' and purports to show a couple *in flagrante delicto*. It's sillier and more fun than other erotic museums in the Red Light District. Minimum age for entry is 16. (www.sexmuseumamsterdam.nl;

Damrak 18; admission €4; 🕙9.30am-11.30pm; 🚊1/2/5/13/17 Centraal Station)

Cannabis College CULTURAL CENTRE

10 👁 Map p26, D5

This nonprofit centre offers visitors tips and tricks for having a positive smoking experience, as well as provides the low-down on local cannabis laws. Browse displays, try out a vaporiser (€3; bring your own smoking material) or view marijuana plants growing sky-high in the basement garden (€3; photos permitted). (📞423 44 20; www.cannabiscollege.com; Oudezijds Achterburgwal 124; 🕙11am-7pm; 🚊4/9/16/24 Dam)

Eating

Gartine CAFE €

11 🍴 Map p26, B7

Gartine is magical, from its covert location in an alley off busy Kalverstraat to its mismatched antique tableware and its sublime breakfast pastries, sandwiches and salads (made from produce grown in its garden plot). The sweet-and-savoury high tea is a scrumptious bonus. (📞320 41 32; www.gartine.nl; Taksteeg 7; mains €6-12, high tea €16-25; 🕙10am-6pm Wed-Sun; 🍴; 🚊4/9/14/16/24 Spui/Rokin)

Vleminckx FAST FOOD €

12 🍴 Map p26, B8

Vleminckx has been frying up *frites* (French fries) since 1887, and doing it at this hole-in-the-wall takeaway

Understand
Red Light District & Legalised Prostitution

As much as the tourism board wishes it weren't so, the Red Light District – aka De Wallen (The Quays) – is a distinguishing feature of Amsterdam. Perhaps what's most fascinating is that it's not a festering den of sleaze. Granted, lads on lost weekends don't set a great tone, but this may be the safest vice zone in the world.

No Big Deal
To the Dutch, legal prostitution is simply an industry like any other. Still, it's mind-bending when you first set eyes on the women in the windows, illuminated not only with red lights (because it's the most flattering hue), but also with black ones that make their white lingerie glow enticingly. Your first instinct might be to take a photo, but don't do it – out of simple respect, and to avoid having your camera tossed in a canal by the ladies' enforcers.

You'll see specialisation – an NL sticker in a window, indicating 'Dutch spoken here', and sections occupied by women from Africa, Eastern Europe or Asia – and of course aggressive self-marketing. Women pay to rent a window typically for an eight-hour shift; they also pay income taxes.

An intriguing place to view the action is Trompettersteeg, a metre-wide alley where some of the most desirable women are stationed. Look for the entrance in the block south of the Oude Kerk.

Clean-Up
Over the past few years, city officials have reduced the number of windows in an effort to clean up the district. They claim it's not about morals but about crime: pimps, traffickers and money launderers have entered the scene and set the neighbourhood on a downward spiral. Clean-up opponents point to a growing conservatism and say the government is using crime as an excuse, because it doesn't like Amsterdam's reputation for sin.

As the window tally decreases, fashion studios, art galleries and trendy cafes rise up to reclaim the deserted spaces, thanks to a program of low-cost rent and other business incentives. To date, more than a fifth of the 482 windows have been shut down.

shack near the Spui for more than 50 years. The standard is smothered in mayonnaise, though you can also ask for ketchup, peanut sauce or a variety of spicy toppings. (http://vleminckxdesausmeester.nl; Voetboogstraat 31; fries €2.10-4.10, sauces €0.60; ⊙noon-7pm Sun & Mon, 11am-7pm Tue, Wed, Fri & Sat, to 8pm Thu; 🚊1/2/5 Koningsplein)

De Laatste Kruimel   CAFE €

13 🍴 Map p26, B7

Hmm, what to look at first: the uber-cute interior decorated with vintage objects from the Noordermarkt and the recycled pallets being used as furniture? Or the glass cases stacked with pies, quiches, breads, cakes and lemon poppyseed scones. Grandmothers, children, couples on dates and just about everyone else pack the 'Last Crumb' for the fantastic organic sandwiches and treats. (📞423 04 99; www.delaatstekruimel.nl; Langebrugsteeg 4; mains

---

Local Life
Rob Wigboldus Vishandel

A wee three-table oasis that's veiled by the surrounding tourist tat, **Rob Wigboldus Vishandel** (📞626 33 88; Zoutsteeg 6; sandwiches €2.50-4.50; ⊙9am-5pm Tue-Sat; 🚊4/9/16/24 Dam) is an authentic spot to sample one of the city's best local bites: fresh herring. The shop serves the fish on a choice of crusty white or brown rolls, with onions and pickles on top.

€2-9; ⊙8am-8pm Mon-Sat, 9am-8pm Sun; 🚊4/9/14/16/24 Spui/Rokin)

Thais Snackbar Bird   THAI €€

14 🍴 Map p26, E4

Don't tell the Chinese neighbours, but this is some of the best Asian food on the Zeedijk – the cooks, wedged in a tiny kitchen, don't skimp on lemongrass, fish sauce or chilli. The resulting curries and basil-laden meat and seafood dishes will knock your socks off. (📞420 62 89; www.thai-bird.nl; Zeedijk 77; mains €9-16; ⊙2-10pm; 🚊4/9/16/24 Centraal Station)

Blauw aan de Wal   INTERNATIONAL €€€

15 🍴 Map p26, D5

Definitely a rose among thorns: a long, often graffiti-covered hallway in the middle of the Red Light District leads to this Garden of Eden. Originally a 17th-century herb warehouse, the whitewashed, exposed-brick, multilevel space still features old steel weights and measures, plus friendly, knowledgeable service and refined French- and Italian-inspired cooking. In summer grab a table in the romantic garden. (📞330 22 57; www.blauwaandewal.com; Oudezijds Achterburgwal 99; 3-/4-course menu €55/67.50; ⊙6-11.30pm Tue-Sat; 🚊4/9/16/24 Dam)

Van Kerkwijk   INTERNATIONAL €€

16 🍴 Map p26, C6

Van Kerkwijk is so low-key you might not notice it, but locals sure know

Oude Kerk (p28)

it's there; the small wooden tables are typically packed. It doesn't take reservations, and there's no menu, so you'll have to wait for the server to tell you what's available that day: perhaps an Indonesian curry, a North African tagine, or various French and Italian meaty classics. (www.caferestaurantvankerkwijk.nl; Nes 41; mains €16-24; ☺11am-1am; 🚊4/9/16/24 Dam)

Haesje Claes
DUTCH €€

17 🍴 Map p26, A7

Haesje Claes' warm surrounds – a tad touristy, but with lots of dark wood and antique knick-knacks – are just the place to sample comforting pea soup and *stamppot* (mashed pot: pota-toes mashed with another vegetable). The fish starter has a great sampling of different Dutch fish. (☎624 99 98; www.haesjeclaes.nl; Spuistraat 273-275; mains €16-26; set menus from €32.50; ☺noon-10pm; 🚊1/2/5 Spui)

'Skek
CAFE €€

18 🍴 Map p26, D3

Run by students for students (flashing your ID gets you 25% off), this friendly cafe-bar is an excellent place to get fat sandwiches on thick slices of multigrain bread, and healthy main dishes with chicken, fish or pasta. Bands occasionally perform at night (the bar stays open to 1am weekdays, and 3am on weekends). (☎427 05 51;

Dam Square (p30)

www.skek.nl; Zeedijk 4-8; sandwiches €4-7,
mains €12-14; ⏲4-10pm Mon, noon-10pm
Tue-Sun; 🛜; 🚃4/9/16/24 Centraal Station)

Tomaz
FRENCH, DUTCH €€

19 🍴 Map p26, B7

Charming little Tomaz hides near the
Begijnhof, and is a fine spot for a light
lunch or informal dinner, accompanied
by a bottle of wine, of course. A vegetarian special is always available. Linger
for a while over a game of chess. (📞320
64 89; www.tomaz.nl; Begijnensteeg 6-8; mains
€15-20; ⏲noon-10pm; 🍴; 🚃1/2/5 Spui)

Anna
MODERN DUTCH €€€

20 🍴 Map p26, C4

It's quite a contrast: Anna's sleek line
of white-clothed tables topped by

plates of curry-sauced monkfish and
truffle-and-veal risotto, while steps
away the world's oldest profession is in
full swing. The restaurant sits right by
the Oude Kerk and the active Red Light
windows surrounding it. A robust list of
organic and global wines complements
the brilliantly executed fare. (📞428 11
11; www.restaurantanna.nl; Warmoesstraat 111;
mains €19-26, 4-course menu €47.50; ⏲6-
10.30pm Mon-Sat; 🚃4/9/16/24 Dam)

Dwaze Zaken
CAFE €€

21 🍴 Map p26, D3

A refuge from red-light madness, this
mosaic-trimmed corner cafe has big
windows and a menu of spicy sandwiches, veggie-rich soups and creative
fondue. A fine selection of beer (with
an emphasis on Belgian elixirs) helps
wash it down. Jazzy live music adds to
the vibe on Mondays, when there are
€7 dinners as well. (📞612 41 75; www.dwa
zezaken.nl; Prins Hendrikkade 50; sandwiches
€7-8, mains €17-20; ⏲9am-midnight Mon-Sat,
to 5.30pm Sun; 🚃4/9/16/24 Centraal Station)

Drinking

Wynand Fockink
TASTING HOUSE

22 🍷 Map p26, C5

This small tasting house (dating from
1679) serves scores of *jenever* (gin) and
liqueurs in an arcade behind Grand
Hotel Krasnapolsky. Although there
are no seats or stools, it's an intimate
place to knock back a shot glass or
two. Guides give an English-language
tour of the distillery and tastings (six

samples) on weekends at 3pm, 4.30pm, 6pm and 7.30pm (€17.50, reservations not required). (www.wynand-fockink.nl; Pijlsteeg 31; ⏱3-9pm; 🚊4/9/16/24 Dam)

Hoppe
BROWN CAFÉ

23 🚊 Map p26, A8

Gritty Hoppe has been filling glasses for more than 340 years. Journalists, barflies, socialites and raconteurs toss back brews amid the ancient wood panelling. Most months the energetic crowd spews out from the dark interior and onto the Spui. Note Hoppe has two parts: the traditional brown *café* and a modern pub with a terrace, located next door (to the left). (www.cafehoppe.com; Spui 18-20; ⏱8am-1am; 🚊1/2/5 Spui)

In 't Aepjen
BROWN CAFÉ

24 🚊 Map p26, E3

Candles burn even during the day at this bar based in a mid-16th-century house, which is one of two remaining wooden buildings in the city. The name allegedly comes from the bar's role in the 16th and 17th centuries as a crash pad for sailors from the Far East, who often toted *aapjes* (monkeys) with them. (Zeedijk 1; ⏱noon-1am Mon-Thu, to 3am Fri & Sat; 🚊4/9/16/24 Centraal Station)

Café Belgique
BEER CAFÉ

25 🚊 Map p26, B4

Pull up a stool at the carved wooden bar and pick from the glinting brass taps. It's all about Belgian beers here, as you may have surmised. Eight flow

from the spouts, and 30 or so more are available in bottles. The ambience is quintessential *gezellig* (convivial, cosy) and draws lots of chilled-out locals. There's live music and DJs some nights. (www.cafe-belgique.nl; Gravenstraat 2; ⏱3pm-1am; 🚊1/9/16/24 Dam)

Café de Dokter
BROWN CAFÉ

26 🚊 Map p26, B7

Very atmospheric and slightly spooky, Café de Dokter is said to be Amsterdam's smallest pub. Candles flicker on the tables, music from old jazz records drifts in the background, and a couple of centuries of dust drapes over the chandeliers and birdcage hanging

☑ Top Tip

Café vs Coffeeshop

There's a big difference between a *café* and a coffeeshop. To wit: '*café*' means 'pub' throughout the Netherlands; a 'coffeeshop' is where one procures marijuana. The latter probably serves coffee, but the focus is on cannabis. Alcohol is not permitted.

On the other hand, *cafés* are cheery, beery local hang-outs, where denizens spend hours reading, chatting with friends and snacking. Traditional *bruin cafés* (brown cafes) – named for the centuries of smoke stains on the walls – are the genre's crowning glory. Visiting one of these cosy, candlelit nirvanas is an Amsterdam must.

from the ceiling. Whiskies and smoked beef sausage are the specialities, but good beers flow, too. (☏ 626 44 27; www. cafe-de-dokter.nl; Rozenboomsteeg 4; ⏰ 4pm-1am Tue-Sat; ⛴ 1/2/5 Spui)

In de Olofspoort TASTING HOUSE

27 🚇 Map p26, D3

The door of this brown *café*–tasting room was once the city gate. A crew of regulars has *jenever* bottles stocked just for them. Check out the jaw-dropping selection behind the back-room bar. Occasional singalongs add to the atmosphere. (☏ 624 39 18; www.olofspoort. com; Nieuwebrugsteeg 13; ⏰ 4pm-12.30am Tue-Thu, 3pm-1.30am Fri & Sat, 3-10pm Sun; ⛴ 4/9/16/24 Centraal Station)

Dampkring COFFEESHOP

28 🚇 Map p26, B8

With an interior that resembles a larger-than-life lava lamp, Damp-kring is a consistent Cannabis Cup winner, and known for having the

---

☑️ Top Tip

How to Drink Jenever

You're at the local tasting house, and you've ordered a *jenever* (akin to gin). It arrives in a tulip-shaped shot glass filled to the brim. You can't pick it up without spilling it. What to do? Bend over the bar, with your hands behind your back, and take a deep sip. That's what tradition dictates.

---

most comprehensive menu in town (including details about smell, taste and effect). Its name references the ring of the earth's atmosphere where smaller items combust. (www.dampkring-coffeeshop-amsterdam.nl; Handboogstraat 29; ⏰ 10am-1am; 📶; ⛴ 1/2/5 Koningsplein)

't Mandje GAY

29 🚇 Map p26, E4

Amsterdam's oldest gay bar opened in 1927, then shut in 1982, when the Zeedijk grew too seedy. But its trinket-covered interior was lovingly dusted every week until it reopened in 2008. The devoted bartenders can tell you stories about the bar's brassy lesbian founder. It's one of the most *gezellig* places in the centre, gay or straight. (www.cafetmandje.nl; Zeedijk 63; ⏰ 5pm-1am Tue-Thu, 4pm-1am Fri, 3pm-1am Sat & Sun; ⛴ 4/9/16/24 Centraal Station)

Brouwerij De Prael BEER CAFÉ

30 🚇 Map p26, D3

Sample organic beers (Scotch ale, IPA, barleywine and many more varieties) at the multilevel tasting room of socially minded De Prael brewery, known for employing people with a history of mental illness. A mostly younger crowd hoists suds and forks into well-priced stews and other Dutch standards at the comfy couches and big wood tables strewn about. There's often live music. (☏ 408 44 69; www.deprael.nl; Oudezijds Armsteeg 26; ⏰ noon-midnight Mon-Wed, to 1am Thu-Sat, to 11pm Sun; ⛴ 4/9/16/24 Centraal Station)

Understand

The Smoking Low-Down

Cannabis is not *technically* legal in the Netherlands – yet it is widely tolerated. Here's the deal: the possession and purchase of small amounts (5g) of 'soft drugs' (ie marijuana, hashish, space cakes and mushroom-based truffles) is allowed, and users aren't prosecuted for smoking or carrying this amount. This means that coffeeshops are actually conducting an illegal business – but again, it is tolerated to a certain extent.

Products for Sale

Most cannabis products sold in the Netherlands used to be imported, but today the country has high-grade home produce, so-called *nederwiet*. It's a particularly strong product – the most potent varieties contain 15% tetrahydrocannabinol (THC), the active substance that gets people high (since 2011, anything above 15% is classified as a hard drug and therefore illegal). In a nutshell, Dutch weed will literally blow your mind – perhaps to an extent that isn't altogether pleasant. Newbies to smoking pot and hash should exercise caution. Space cakes and cookies (baked goods made with hash or marijuana) are also sold in coffeeshops. Most shops offer rolling papers, pipes or bongs to use; you can also buy ready-made joints.

Dos & Don'ts

Do ask coffeeshop staff for advice on what and how to consume, and heed it, even if nothing happens after an hour. And do ask staff for the menu of products on offer. Conversely, don't drink alcohol (it's illegal in coffeeshops), and don't smoke tobacco, whether mixed with marijuana or on its own. It is forbidden in accordance with the Netherlands' laws.

Coffeeshop Closures

In some areas of the country, foreigners are banned from coffeeshops. Not so in Amsterdam. The city's authorities are often at odds with their national counterparts when it comes to restrictive policies, as coffeeshops are a big part of Amsterdam's tourism business, with around one-third of travellers visiting the smoky venues. Nonetheless, a few dozen have closed recently as rules went into effect that shut down coffeeshops operating near schools. More than 150 Amsterdam coffeeshops still remain open for business.

Winston Kingdom
CLUB

31 😃 Map p26, C4

This is a club that even nonclubbers will love for its indie-alternative music beats, smiling DJs and stiff drinks. No matter what's on – from 'dubstep mayhem' to Thailand-style full-moon parties – the scene can get pretty wild in this good-time space. (www.winston.nl; Warmoesstraat 127, Hotel Winston; ⏰9pm-4am Sun-Thu, to 5am Fri & Sat; 🚊4/9/16/24 Dam)

Greenhouse
COFFEESHOP

32 😃 Map p26, C6

This is one of the most popular coffeeshops in town. Smokers love the funky music, multicoloured mosaics, psychedelic stained-glass windows and high-quality weed and hash. It also serves breakfast, lunch and dinner to suit all levels of the munchies. It's mostly a young, backpacking crowd partaking of the wares. (www.greenhouse.org; Oudezijds Voorburgwal 191; ⏰9am-1am; 🛜; 🚊4/9/16/24 Dam)

> Local Life
>
> **Tweede Kamer**
>
> Teeny, wood-panelled **Tweede Kamer** (📞422 22 36; Heisteeg 6; ⏰10am-1am; 🚊1/2/5 Spui) feels more like a brown *café* than a coffeeshop. But weed there is, and the selection is vast. It's mostly locals creating the billows of smoke that spill out the door. The Sativa is highly recommended for a special happy high.

Entertainment

Bitterzoet
LIVE MUSIC

33 ⭐ Map p26, C2

Always full, always changing, this is one of the friendliest venues in town. One night it might be full of skater dudes; the next, relaxed 30-somethings. Music (sometimes live, sometimes a DJ) can be funk, roots, drum'n'bass, Latin, Afrobeat, old-school jazz or hip-hop groove. (www.bitterzoet.com; Spuistraat 2; ⏰8pm-late; 🚊1/2/5/13/17 Nieuwezijds Kolk)

Casa Rosso
LIVE PERFORMANCE

34 ⭐ Map p26, D5

It might be stretching it to describe a live sex show as 'classy,' but this theatre is clean and comfortable and always packed with couples and hen's-night parties. Acts can be male, female, both or lesbian (although not gay...sorry boys!). Performers demonstrate everything from positions of the Kama Sutra to pole dances and incredible tricks with lit candles. (www.casarosso.nl; Oudezijds Achterburgwal 106-108; admission with/without drinks €50/40; ⏰7pm-2am; 🚊4/9/16/24 Dam)

Frascati
THEATRE

35 ⭐ Map p26, B7

This experimental theatre is a draw for young Dutch directors, choreographers and producers. Expect multicultural dance and music performances, as well as hip hop, rap and breakdancing. Check the website for upcoming events. (📞626 68 66; www.frascatitheater.nl; Nes 63; 🕐closed Aug; 🚊4/9/14/16/24 Spui/Rokin)

De Brakke Grond
THEATRE

36 ⭐ Map p26, C6

De Brakke Grond sponsors a fantastic array of music, experimental video, modern dance and exciting young theatre at its nifty performance hall. Visit the website to find out about upcoming events. (📞626 68 66; www. brakkegrond.nl; Nes 45, Flemish Cultural Centre; 🚊4/9/14/16/24 Spui/Rokin)

Shopping

Condomerie Het Gulden Vlies
GIFTS

37 🔵 Map p26, C5

Perfectly positioned for the Red Light District, this boutique sells condoms in every imaginable size, colour, flavour and design (horned devils, marijuana leaves, Delftware tiles…), along with lubricants and saucy gifts. (www.condo merie.com; Warmoesstraat 141; 🕐11am-6pm Mon-Sat, 1-5pm Sun; 🚊4/9/14/16/24 Dam)

American Book Center
BOOKS

38 🔵 Map p26, A7

This excellent three-storey shop is the biggest source of English-language books in Amsterdam. Its greatest strengths are in the artsy ground-floor department, but on the upper floors there's fiction and special-interest titles,

✅ Top Tip
Magic Truffles

Psilocybin mushrooms are banned in the Netherlands, but trippy magic truffles are legal. They're widely available at 'smart shops', which deal in organic uppers and natural hallucinogens. Counter staff advise on the nuances of dosages and possible effects, as if at a pharmacy. Listen to them. Every year, emergency-room nurses have to sit with people on bad trips brought on by consuming more than the recommended amount. Also, it seems obvious, but never buy truffles or other drugs on the street.

plus a travel section. It also stocks foreign periodicals such as the *New York Times*. Top-notch postcards, too! (ABC; www.abc.nl; Spui 12; 🕐noon-8pm Mon, 10am-8pm Tue-Sat, 11am-6.30pm Sun; 🚊1/2/5 Spui)

PGC Hajenius
GIFTS

39 🔵 Map p26, B7

Even if you're not a cigar connoisseur, this tobacco emporium is worth a browse. Inside is all art-deco stained glass, gilt trim and soaring ceilings. Regular customers, including members of the Dutch royal family, have private humidors here. You can sample your Cuban stogie and other exotic purchases in the handsome smoking lounge. (www.hajenius.com; Rokin 96; 🕐noon-6pm Mon, 9.30am-6pm Tue-Sat, noon-5pm Sun; 🚊4/9/14/16/24 Spui/Rokin)

Kokopelli

SMART SHOP

40 Map p26, D3

Were it not for its trade in 'magic truffles' (similar to the now-outlawed psilocybin mushrooms, aka 'magic mushrooms') you might swear this large, beautiful space was a fashionable clothing or homewares store. There's a coffee and juice bar and a chill-out lounge area overlooking Damrak. (www.kokopelli.nl; Warmoesstraat 12; ☺11am-10pm; 🚊4/9/16/24 Centraal Station)

De Bijenkorf

DEPARTMENT STORE

41 🔒 Map p26, B5

The city's most fashionable department store is in the highest-profile location, facing the Royal Palace. Design-conscious shoppers will enjoy the well-chosen clothing, toys, household accessories and books. It's a good place to stop in to use the bathrooms, which are free. The very snazzy cafe on the 5th floor has a terrace with steeple views. (www.debijenkorf.nl; Dam 1; ☺11am-8pm Sun & Mon, 10am-8pm Tue & Wed, to 9pm Thu & Fri, 9.30am-8pm Sat; 🚊4/9/16/24 Dam)

Hema

DEPARTMENT STORE

42 🔒 Map p26, C4

What used to be the nation's equivalent of Marks & Spencer, Woolworths or Target now attracts as many design aficionados as bargain hunters. Expect low prices, reliable quality and a wide range of products, including good-value wines and delicatessen goods. (www.hema.nl; Nieuwendijk 174; ☺9am-7pm Mon-Fri, to 6pm Sat, noon-6pm Sun; 🚊4/9/16/24 Dam)

Gastronomie Nostalgie

HOMEWARES

43 🔒 Map p26, A7

The owner scours auctions in Paris and other cities for the gorgeous china plates, crystal goblets, silver candlesticks and other antique homewares spilling out of this jam-packed shop. Ring the brass bell to get in, then prepare to browse for a good long while. (www.gastronomienostalgie.nl; 304 Nieuwezijds Voorburgwal; ☺11am-5pm; 🚊1/2/5 Spui)

By Popular Demand

GIFTS

44 🔒 Map p26, A5

Stop in this large, sunny shop for nifty gift-y items. Cool cards, groovy

BIRUTE / GETTY IMAGES ©

Museum Ons' Lieve Heer op Solder (p28)

gadgets and hip lamps and other home decor stock the shelves. Many items are pocket-sized, so travellers can find original, easy-to-transport souvenirs. The wares are infinitely browsable. (☎624 52 31; Raadhuisstraat 2; ⏰10am-7pm Mon-Sat, 11am-7pm Sun; 🚊4/9/16/24 Dam)

Mr B
ACCESSORIES

45 🔒 Map p26, D4

Kinky! The tamer wares at this renowned Red Light District shop include leather and rubber suits, hoods and bondage equipment, all of which can be made to measure if you want. Horny toys add a playful (and somewhat scary) element. (www.misterb. com; Warmoesstraat 89; ⏰10.30am-7pm Mon-Wed & Fri, to 9pm Thu, 11am-6pm Sat, 1-6pm Sun; 🚊4/9/16/24 Dam)

RoB
ACCESSORIES

46 🔒 Map p26, D4

RoB sells anything and everything for one's bondage and rough-sex fantasy: army gear, leather and rubber are just the start. Items ranging from the 'Adonis pouch' to the 'black stretchy ring' stock the shelves. (www.rob.eu; Warmoesstraat 71; ⏰11am-7pm Mon-Sat, 1-6pm Sun; 🚊4/9/16/24 Centraal Station)

Explore

Jordaan & Western Canals

If Amsterdam's neighbourhoods held a 'best personality' contest, the Jordaan would surely win. Its intimacy is contagious, with jovial bar singalongs, beery *bruin cafés* (pubs) and flower-box-adorned eateries spilling out onto the narrow streets. The Western Canals flow next door. Grand old buildings and oddball little speciality shops line the glinting waterways. Roaming around them can cause days to vanish.

The Sights in a Day

☀ Do the Dutch thing and carve into a hulking pancake at, well, **Pancakes!** (p56). Poke around the surrounding shops, then cross over Prinsengracht to see what life on the water is like at the **Houseboat Museum** (p51).

☀ Devote the afternoon to the neighbourhood's gorgeous canals. Visit **Het Grachtenhuis** (p50), which tells the story of the 400-year-old waterways and their engineering genius. Afterward walk along the Herengracht and ogle the Golden Age manors rising up along the canal. Munch an opulent canal-side lunch at **De Belhamel** (p54). Photography buffs can see what's on at **Huis Marseille** (p51).

☾ Head over to the **Anne Frank Huis** (p44) in the early evening, when crowds are thinnest. For dinner, head to mod-rustic **Balthazar's Keuken** (p52) for whatever the daily special is, or have a leisurely Afghan meal at **Mantoe** (p55). Then take your pick of brown *cafés* for a nightcap. **'t Smalle** (p56) always hosts a high-spirited group. Or croon with the crowd at **De Twee Zwaantjes** (p57).

For a local's day in the Jordaan & Western Canals, see p46.

👁 Top Sights
Anne Frank Huis (p44)

🔍 Local Life
Shopping the Jordaan & Western Canals (p46)

♥ Best of Amsterdam

Eating
Bistro Bij Ons (p54)

Drinking & Nightlife
't Smalle (p56)

La Tertulia (p58)

Shopping
Noordermarkt (p47)

Frozen Fountain (p60)

Moooi Gallery (p61)

Tenue de Nîmes (p62)

SPRMRKT (p63)

Antiekcentrum Amsterdam (p46)

Getting There

🚊 **Tram** For the Western Canals, trams 13, 14 and 17 stop near the shops and top sights; trams 1, 2 and 5 to the Spui are also just a short walk away. For the Jordaan, tram 10 along Marnixstraat is your best bet for the neighbourhood's western edge; trams 13 and 14 along Rozengracht go through the centre.

Top Sights
Anne Frank Huis

It is one of the 20th century's most compelling stories: a young Jewish girl forced into hiding with her family and their friends to escape deportation by the Nazis. The house they used as a hideaway attracts nearly one million visitors a year. Walking through the bookcase-door of the Secret Annexe and into the claustrophobic living quarters is to step back into a time that seems both distant and tragically real.

Anne Frank House

👁 Map p48, C4

☏ 556 71 00

www.annefrank.org

Prinsengracht 267

adult/child €9/4.50

🕗 9am-9pm, hours vary seasonally

🚊 13/14/17 Westermarkt

Photos of Anne Frank in Anne Frank Huis

Don't Miss

The Occupants

The Franks – father Otto, mother Edith, older sister Margot and Anne – moved into the hidden chambers in July 1942, along with Mr and Mrs van Pels (whom Anne called the van Daans in her diary) and their son Peter. Four months later Fritz Pfeffer (aka Albert van Dussel) joined the household. The group lived there until they were mysteriously betrayed to the Gestapo in August 1944.

Offices & Warehouse

The building originally held Otto Frank's pectin (a substance used in jelly-making) business. On the lower floors you'll see the former offices of Victor Kugler, Otto's business partner; and the desks of Miep Gies, Bep Voskuijl and Jo Kleiman, all of whom worked in the office and provided food, clothing and other goods for the household.

Secret Annexe

The upper floors in the *achterhuis* (rear house) contain the Secret Annexe, where the living quarters have been preserved in powerful austerity. As you enter Anne's small bedroom, you can still sense the remnants of a young girl's dreams: view the photos of Hollywood stars and postcards of the Dutch royal family she pasted on the wall.

The Diary

More haunting exhibits and videos await after you return to the front house – including Anne's red-plaid diary itself, sitting alone in its glass case. Watch the video of Anne's old schoolmate Hanneli Gosler, who describes encountering Anne at Bergen-Belsen. Read heartbreaking letters from Otto, the only Secret Annexe occupant to survive the concentration camps.

☑ Top Tips

▶ Come after 6pm to avoid the biggest crowds. Queues can easily be an hour-plus wait otherwise.

▶ Buying timed-entry tickets in advance allows you to skip the queue entirely and enter via a separate door (left of the main entrance).

▶ Prebook via the museum's website (€0.50 surcharge), though you must buy the tickets several days ahead of time and be able to print them or show them on your smartphone.

▶ You can also prebook via the visitor centre at Centraal Station (€1 surcharge) on shorter notice (three days or so).

✗ Take a Break

The museum cafe offers apple pie and canal views. For pancakes, sandwiches and 18th-century atmosphere aplenty, stroll over to 't Smalle (p56).

Local Life
Shopping the Jordaan & Western Canals

These are Amsterdam's prime neighbourhoods to stumble upon offbeat little shops selling items you'd find nowhere else. Velvet ribbons? Herb-spiced Gouda? Vintage jewellery? They're all here amid the Western Canals' quirky stores and the Jordaan's eclectic boutiques and markets. Everything is squashed into a grid of tiny lanes – a perfect place to lose yourself for an afternoon stroll.

❶ Antiquing at Antiekcentrum

Anyone who likes peculiar old stuff might enter **Antiekcentrum Amsterdam** (Amsterdam Antique Centre; www.antiekcentrumamsterdam. nl; Elandsgracht 109; ⊙11am-6pm Mon & Wed-Fri, to 5pm Sat & Sun; ⊕7/10/17 Elandsgracht), a knick-knack minimall, and never come out. You're just as likely to find 1940s silk dresses as you are 1970s

Swedish porn. Brasserie Blazer serves well-priced French fare inside to fuel the browsing.

2 Tunes at Johnny Jordaanplein

The small square **Johnny Jordaanplein** (cnr Prinsengracht & Elandsgracht; 🚊13/14/17 Westermarkt) is dedicated to the local hero and musician who sang the romantic music known as *levenslied* (tears-in-your-beer-style ballads). There are bronze busts of Johnny and his band, but the real star here is the colourful utility hut splashed with nostalgic lyrics.

3 Wander the Negen Straatjes

The **Negen Straatjes** (Nine Streets; www.de9straatjes.nl; 🚊1/2/5 Spui) comprise a tic-tac-toe board of wee shops dealing in vintage fashions, housewares and oddball specialities from toothbrushes to antique eyeglass frames. It's bordered by Reestraat, Hartenstraat and Gasthuismolensteeg to the north and Runstraat, Huidenstraat and Wijde Heisteeg to the south. Bonus points if you find the doll doctor!

4 Munch at Lunchcafé Nielsen

Looking for where the locals go to lunch and brunch in the Negen Straatjes? **Lunchcafé Nielsen** (📞330 60 06; Berenstraat 19; mains €5-11; ⏰8am-4pm Tue-Fri, to 6pm Sat, 9am-5pm Sun; 🍴; 🚊13/14/17 Westermarkt) it is. Under leafy murals, chow on hearty quiches, salads, and fresh lemon and apple cakes that disappear as quickly as they're put out.

5 Rummage the Noordermarkt

The **Noordermarkt** (Northern Market; www.jordaanmarkten.nl; Noordermarkt; ⏰flea market 9am-1pm Mon, farmers market 9am-4pm Sat; 🚊3/10 Marnixplein) surrounds the Noorderkerk and hosts two bazaars. On Monday mornings it's a trove of secondhand clothing (great rummage piles) and assorted antique trinkets. On Saturdays, most of the clothing stalls are replaced by gorgeous produce and *kaas* (cheese) from growers around Amsterdam.

6 Get Hip on Haarlemmerdijk

The street **Haarlemmerdijk** buzzes with stylish shops and lots of places to snack or unwind over a drink. It is a culinary destination, not just for restaurants but for its slew of gourmet provisions and kitchen shops. Keep an eye out for hip lolly makers, cookbook vendors and tea emporiums among the retailers.

7 Relax at De Kat in de Wijngaert

De Kat in de Wijngaert (📞620 45 54; www.dekatindewijngaert.nl; Lindengracht 160; ⏰10am-1am Sun-Thu, 10am-3am Fri, 9am-3am Sat; 🚊3/10 Marnixplein) is the kind of brown *café* where one beer soon turns into half a dozen – maybe it's the influence of the old-guard arts types who hang out here. Try soaking it up with what many people vote as the best *tosti* (toasted sandwich) in town.

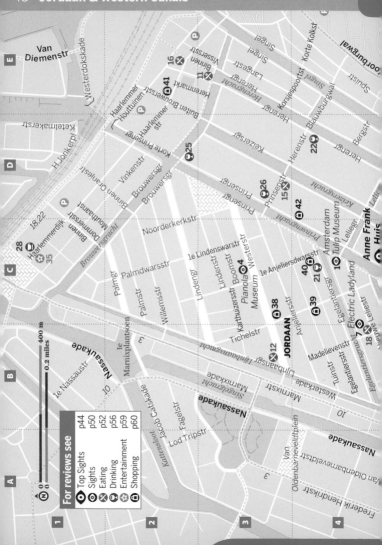

Van Diemenstr

Westerdokskade

Ketelmakerstr

H Jonkerpl

Van Diemenstr

Haarlemmer Houttuinen

Haarlemmerstr

Buiten Brouwersstr

Korte Prinsengr

Binnen Oranjestr

Vinkenstr

Brouwersgr

Brouwersgr

Brouwersgr

Binnen Dommerstr

Haarlemmerdijk

Mouthaanst

Palmgr

Palmdwarsstr

Palmstr

Willemsstr

Palmstr

1e Marnixplantsoen

Nassaukade

1e Nassaustr

1e Nassaustr

1e Nassaukade

Jacob Catskade

Kattenslootl

Lod Tripstr

Noorderkerkstr

1e Lindenswarsstr

1e Lindenswarsstr

Lindengr

Lindenstr

Boomstr

Karthuizersstr

Tichelstr

Singelgracht

Marnixkade

Brouwersgracht

Herengracht

Herenmarkt

Binnen Visserstr

Langestr

Singel

Singel

Korte Kolkst

Heintjeshoek

Korsjespoortst

Singel

Herengr

Herenstr

Herenstr

Keizersgr

Prinsengr

Prinsengr

Prinsengr

Prinsengracht

Lijnbaansgr

Lijnbaansgr

Westerstr

Madelievenstr

Tuinstr

Egelantiersstr

Egelantiersstr

Anjeliersstr

Westerstr

1e Anjeliersdwarsstr

Egelantiersgr

Leliegr

Leliestr

Lelie

Keizersgracht

Blauwburgwal

Bergstr

Herengr

Prinsengracht

Amsterdam Tulip Museum

Anne Frank Huis

Electric Ladyland

JORDAAN

Marnixstr

Westerkade

Westerstr

Singelgracht

Van Oldenbarneveldtstr

Van Oldenbarneveldtplein

Frederik Hendrikstr

Nassaukade

Spuistr

Spuistr

Noordermarkt

Pianola Museum

16

41

11

25

26

15

22

42

28

35

18.22

18.22

4

38

12

40

21

39

18

1

10

3

3

10

0.2 miles

400 m

0 2

N

For reviews see

	Top Sights	p44
	Sights	p50
	Eating	p52
	Drinking	p56
	Entertainment	p59
	Shopping	p60

Sights

Amsterdam Tulip Museum
MUSEUM

1 ⊚ Map p48, C4

Don't be dissuaded – or distracted – by the gift shop overflowing with floral souvenirs at the front of this small museum. And yes, it is small, but the Amsterdam Tulip Museum offers a nifty overview of the history of the country's favourite bloom, and is a fascinating way to spend half an hour or so, especially before taking a day trip to the Keukenhof Flower Gardens or Bloemenveiling Aalsmeer flower auction, or strolling the Southern Canal Ring's Bloemenmarkt (p68). (☑421 00 95; www. amsterdamtulipmuseum.com; Prinsengracht 112; adult/child €5/3; ◷10am-6pm; ⛴13/14/17 Westermarkt)

Het Grachtenhuis
MUSEUM

2 ⊚ Map p48, D7

If you're the kind of person who walks through the Canal Ring and marvels over what a feat of engineering it is, you won't want to miss the Canal House, which explains how the canals and houses that line them were built. The museum uses holograms, videos, models, cartoons and other innovative ways to tell the story. (Canal House; ☑421 16 56; www.hetgrachtenhuis.nl; Herengracht 386; adult/child €12/6; ◷10am-5pm Tue-Sun; ⛴1/2/5 Koningsplein)

Westerkerk
CHURCH

3 ⊚ Map p48, C5

The main gathering place for Amsterdam's Dutch Reformed community, this church was built for rich Protestants to a 1620 design by Hendrick de Keyser. The nave is the largest in the Netherlands and is covered by a wooden barrel vault. The huge main organ dates from 1686, with panels decorated with instruments and biblical scenes. Rembrandt (1606–69), who died bankrupt at nearby Rozengracht, was buried in a pauper's grave somewhere in the church. (Western Church; ☑624 77 66; www. westerkerk.nl; Prinsengracht 281; ◷10am-3pm Mon-Sat; ⛴13/14/17 Westermarkt)

Westerkerk Bell Tower
TOWER

The bell tower of Westerkerk (see 3 ⊚ Map p48, C5) is famously topped by the blue imperial crown that Habsburg emperor Maximilian I bestowed to the city for its coat of arms in 1489. The climb up the stairs of the 85m tower can be strenuous and claustrophobic, but the guide takes breaks on the landings while describing the bells. Tours depart every half-hour. Children under six aren't permitted. (www. westertorenamsterdam.nl; Prinsengracht 281; tours per person €7.50; ◷10am-7.30pm Mon-Sat Apr-Oct)

Pianola Museum
MUSEUM

4 ⊚ Map p48, C3

This is a very special place, crammed with pianolas from the early 1900s.

A canal in the Jordaan area

The museum has around 50 of the instruments, although only a dozen are on display at any given time, as well as some 30,000 music rolls and a player pipe organ. The curator gives an hour-long (or so) guided tour and music demonstrations with great zest. (📞627 96 24; www.pianola.nl; Westerstraat 106; adult/child €5/3; ⏰2-5pm Thu-Sun Jul & Aug, Sun only Sep-Jun; 🚊3/10 Marnixplein)

Houseboat Museum
MUSEUM

5 👁 Map p48, C6

This quirky museum, a 23m-long sailing barge from 1914, offers a good sense of how *gezellig* (cosy) life can be on the water. The actual displays are minimal, but you can watch a presen-

tation on houseboats (some pretty and some ghastly) and inspect the sleeping, living, cooking and dining quarters with all the mod cons. (📞427 07 50; www.houseboatmuseum.nl; Prinsengracht 296k; adult/child €4.50/3.50; ⏰10am-5pm Jul & Aug, Tue-Sun only Mar-Oct, Fri-Sun only Nov-Feb, closed Jan; 🚊13/14/17 Westermarkt)

Huis Marseille
MUSEUM

6 👁 Map p48, C7

This well-curated photography museum stages large-scale, temporary exhibitions, drawing from its own collection as well as hosting travelling shows. Themes might include portraiture, nature or regional photography, spread out over several floors and in a 'summer house' behind the main house. (📞531 89 89; www.huismarseille.nl; Keizersgracht 401; adult/child €8/free; ⏰11am-6pm Tue-Sun; 🚃1/2/5 Keizersgracht)

Electric Ladyland

MUSEUM

7 🎯 Map p48, B4

The world's first museum of fluorescent art features owner Nick Padalino's psychedelic sculpture work on one side and cases of naturally luminescent rocks and manufactured glowing objects (money, government ID cards etc) on the other (his art gallery–shop is upstairs). Jimi Hendrix, the Beatles and other trippy artists play on the stereo while Nick lovingly describes each item in the collection. (www.electric-lady-land.com; 2e Leliedwarsstraat 5; adult/child €5/free; ⏰1-6pm Tue-Sat; 🚃13/14/17 Westermarkt)

Stedelijk Museum Bureau Amsterdam

MUSEUM

8 🎯 Map p48, C5

Don't blink or you might walk right past this unobtrusive outpost, a 'project space' of the Stedelijk Museum (p97). It's in a former clothing workshop on a very quiet block. Exhibits here – from painting and sculpture to new-media and installation pieces – present contemporary artists whose work reflects Amsterdam culture. It's well worth a peek. (📞422 04 71; www.smba.nl; Rozenstraat 59; admission free; ⏰11am-5pm Wed-Sun; 🚃13/14/17 Westermarkt)

Reypenaer Cheese Tasting

COURSE

9 🎯 Map p48, D5

Here's your chance to become a *kaas* (cheese) connoisseur. The 100-plus-year-old Dutch cheese maker Reypenaer offers tastings in a rustic classroom under its shop. The hour-long session includes six cheeses – two goat's milk, four cow's milk – from young to old, with wine and port pairings. Staff will guide you through them, helping you appreciate the cheeses' look, smell and taste. (📞320 63 33; www.reypenaercheese.com; Singel 182; tastings from €15; ⏰tastings by reservation; 🚃1/2/5/13/14/17 Dam/Raadhuisstraat)

Eating

Balthazar's Keuken

MEDITERRANEAN €€

10 🍴 Map p48, B7

In a former blacksmith's forge, with a modern-rustic look, this is consistently one of Amsterdam's top-rated restaurants. Don't expect a wide-ranging menu: the philosophy is basically 'whatever we have on hand', which might mean wild sea bass with mushroom risotto or confit of rabbit, but it's invariably delectable. Reservations recommended. (📞420 21 14; www.balthazarskeuken.nl; Elandsgracht 108; 3-course menu €32.50; ⏰6-10.30pm Wed-Sat; 🚃7/10/17 Elandsgracht)

Understand

Canals

History

In Dutch a canal is a *gracht* (pronounced '*khrakht*'), and the main canals form the central *grachtengordel* (canal ring). These beauties came to life in the early 1600s, after Amsterdam outgrew its medieval walls and city planners put together an ambitious design for expansion. Far from being simply picturesque, or even just waterways for transport, the canals were needed to drain and reclaim the waterlogged land.

Core Canals

Starting from the core, the major semicircular canals are the Singel, Herengracht, Keizersgracht and Prinsengracht. An easy way to remember them is that, apart from the **Singel** (originally a moat that defended Amsterdam's outer limits), these canals are in alphabetical order.

The **Herengracht** is where Amsterdam's wealthiest residents moved once the canals were completed. They named the waterway after the Heeren XVII (17 Gentlemen) of the Dutch East India Company, and built their mansions alongside it. Almost as swanky was the **Keizersgracht** (Emperor's Canal), a nod to Holy Roman Emperor Maximilian I. The **Prinsengracht** – named after William the Silent, Prince of Orange and the first Dutch royal – was designed as a slightly cheaper canal with smaller residences and warehouses. It also acted as a barrier against the crusty working-class quarter beyond, aka the Jordaan. Today the Prinsengracht is the liveliest of Amsterdam's inner canals, with *cafés*, shops and houseboats lining the quays.

Radial Canals

The three major radial canals cut across the core canals like spokes on a bicycle. The **Brouwersgracht** – aka the 'Brewers Canal' – is one of Amsterdam's most beautiful waterways. It takes its name from the many breweries that lined the banks in the 16th and 17th centuries. The **Leidsegracht** was named after the city of Leiden, to which it was the main water route. Peaceful **Reguliersgracht** was named after an order of monks whose monastery was located nearby. In 2010 Unesco dubbed the 400-year-old waterways a World Heritage site.

De Belhamel
FRENCH €€

11 ✗ Map p48, E3

In warm weather the canal-side tables at the head of the Herengracht are an aphrodisiac, and the art-nouveau interior provides the perfect backdrop for superb French- and Italian-inspired dishes such as truffle-parsley-stuffed guinea fowl with polenta; rack of lamb with aubergine biscuit and pepper coulis; or honey- and mustard-marinated veal. (☏622 10 95; www.belhamel.nl; Brouwersgracht 60; mains lunch €15-24.50, dinner €22.50-26.50; ◷noon-4pm & 6-11pm; ☐1/2/5/13/17 Centraal Station)

Restaurant Fraîche
FRENCH €€

12 ✗ Map p48, B3

Cutting-edge French cuisine at this glass-fronted bistro changes seasonally but might include roast turbot and squid with pickled fennel and

smoked carrot purée, or roast duck breast with butterscotch and foie gras sauce. There are various tasting plates too, plus brunch specials. (☏627 99 32; www.restaurantfraiche.nl; Westerstraat 264; mains €17-22; ◷6.30-11.30pm Wed-Sat, noon-4pm Sun; ☐3/10 Marnixplein)

Brasserie Blazer
FRENCH €€

13 ✗ Map p48, B7

Inside the Antiekcentrum Amsterdam (p46) antique centre and opening out onto a narrow canal, Amsterdam's simplest French brasserie is also its most effortlessly sexy, with well-priced classic dishes – *confit de canard* (preserved duck), rib-eye Béarnaise, et al. Try one of the house beers to wash it all down. (☏620 96 90; www. brasserieblazer.nl; Lijnbaansgracht 190; mains €14.50-23.50; ◷kitchen noon-11pm; ☐7/10/17 Elandsgracht)

Bistro Bij Ons
DUTCH €€

14 ✗ Map p48, C5

If you're not in town visiting your Dutch *oma* (grandma), try the honest-to-goodness cooking at this charming retro bistro instead. Classics include *stamppot* (potatoes mashed with another vegetable) with sausage, *raasdonders* (split peas with bacon, onion and pickles) and *poffertjes* (small pancakes with butter and powdered sugar). (☏627 90 16; www. bistrobijons.nl; Prinsengracht 287; mains €13.50-19; ◷10am-10pm Tue-Sun; ♿; ☐13/14/17 Westermarkt)

Q Local Life
Wil Graanstra Friteshuis

Legions of Amsterdammers swear by the crispy spuds at **Wil Graanstra Friteshuis** (☏624 40 71; Westermarkt 11; frites €2.50-4.50; ◷noon-7pm Mon-Sat; ☐13/14/17 Westermarkt). The family-run business has been frying by the Westerkerk since 1956. Most locals top their cones with mayonnaise, though *oorlog* (a peanut sauce–mayo combo), curry sauce and *picalilly* (relish) rock the tastebuds, too.

Letting

DUTCH €

15  Map p48, D3

Start your day in traditional Dutch style with authentic breakfast dishes such as *wentelteefjes* (sugar bread dipped in egg and cinnamon), *uitsmijter rosbief* (eggs served sunny side up, with cheese and roast beef) and scrambled eggs with smoked halibut. At lunch choose from soups and sandwiches. Or book ahead for royal high tea (€25), accompanied by champagne. (www.letting.nl; Prinsenstraat 3; mains €7-13; ⊗8.30am-5pm Mon & Thu-Sat, to 3pm Wed, 9am-5pm Sun; 🖊; 🚊13/14/17 Westermarkt)

Vinnies Deli

CAFE €

16  Map p48, E2

Organic fare at this trendy spot spans sandwiches such as black-bean hummus and sweet peppers, eggplant with buttermilk sauce and pomegranate, and smoked mackerel with rhubarb chutney. Cakes, such as beetroot-topped cheesecake, are equally creative. Self-caterers can pick up the products used in its dishes from the deli. (www. vinniesdeli.nl; Haarlemmerstraat 46; mains €7.50-12.50; ⊗7.30am-6pm Mon-Fri, 9am-6pm Sat, 9.30am-6pm Sun; 🖊👶; 🚊1/2/5/13/17 Centraal Station)

Singel 404

CAFE €

17  Map p48, D7

It's easy to miss this tucked-away spot, despite its location near the bustling Spui (look for the cobalt-blue awning). Sure, the menu is as

Houseboat Museum (p51)

simple as can be – smoked salmon sandwiches, pumpkin soup, honey mint lemonade – but the prices are rock-bottom, portions are generous and the quality is superb. (🌐428 01 54; Singel 404; dishes €5-9; ⊗10.30am-7pm; 🖊; 🚊1/2/5 Spui)

Mantoe

AFGHANI €€

18  Map p48, B4

Settle in for a special meal at Mantoe. An Afghan family runs the small restaurant, which is so snug and friendly it feels like you're eating in someone's home. There is no menu: it's just whatever they cook that day, perhaps steamed dumplings stuffed with minced meat and herbs, or a spicy lamb and rice dish. A good wine list tops it

off. (📞421 63 74; www.restaurantmantoe.
nl; 2e Leliedwarsstraat 13; 4-course menu €32;
🕐5-11pm Wed-Sun; 🚊13/14/17 Westermarkt)

Pancakes!

DUTCH €

19 🍴 Map p48, C6

OK, so maybe it's mostly tourists who
grace the blue-tile tables at snug little
Pancakes!, but who can blame them?
The signature dish rocks, whether it's
sweet (apple, nuts and cinnamon) or
savoury (ham, chicory and Camembert
cheese). The batter is made with flour
sourced from a local mill. Gluten-free
pancakes are also available. (📞528 97
97; www.pancakesamsterdam.com; Berenstraat 38; pancakes €9.50-12.50; 🕐9am-
7pm; 🛜🍴👶; 🚊13/14/17 Westermarkt)

Understand
Drop the Liquorice

The Dutch love their lollies, the
most famous of which is *drop*, the
word for all varieties of liquorice.
It may be gummy-soft or tough
as leather, shaped like coins or
miniature cars, but the most
important distinction is between
zoete (sweet) and *zoute* (salty,
also called *salmiak*). The latter is
often an alarming surprise, even for
avowed fans of the black stuff. But
with such a range of textures and
additional flavours – mint, honey,
laurel – even liquorice-sceptics
might be converted. Het Oud-
Hollandsch Snoepwinkeltje (p61) is
a good place to do a taste test.

Moeders

DUTCH €€

20 🍴 Map p48, A6

Mum's the word at 'Mothers'. When
this welcoming place opened in 1990
customers were asked to bring their
own plates and photos of their mums
as donations and the decor remains
a delightful hotchpotch. So does the
food, from pumpkin *stamppot* (potatoes mashed with pumpkin) to seafood
and Moroccan dishes. Book ahead.
(📞626 79 57; www.moeders.com; Rozengracht
251; mains €15-19, 3-course menus from
€26.50; 🕐5pm-midnight Mon-Fri, from noon
Sat & Sun; 👶; 🚊13/14/17 Marnixstraat)

Drinking

't Smalle

BROWN CAFÉ

21 🍺 Map p48, C4

Dating back to 1786 as a *jenever* (Dutch
gin) distillery and tasting house, and
restored during the 1970s with antique
porcelain beer pumps and lead-framed
windows, locals' favourite 't Smalle is
one of Amsterdam's charming brown
cafés. Dock your boat right by the
pretty stone terrace, which is wonderfully convivial by day and impossibly
romantic at night. (www.t-smalle.nl;
Egelantiersgracht 12; 🕐10am-1am Sun-Thu, to
2am Fri & Sat; 🚊13/14/17 Westermarkt)

't Arendsnest

BEER CAFÉ

22 🍺 Map p48, D4

This gorgeous, restyled brown *café,*
with its glowing copper *jenever*
boilers behind the bar, only serves

Dutch beer – but with nearly 200 varieties (many of them from small breweries), including 30 on tap, you'll need to move here to try them all. (www.arendsnest.nl; Herengracht 90; ⊗noon-midnight Sun-Thu, to 2am Fri & Sat; 🚃1/2/5/13/17 Nieuwezijds Kolk)

Cafe Soundgarden BAR

23 🚇 Map p48, A6

In this grungy, all-ages dive bar, the 'Old Masters' are the Ramones and Black Sabbath. Somehow a handful of pool tables, 1980s pinball machines, unkempt DJs and lovably surly bartenders add up to an ineffable magic. Bands occasionally make an appearance, and the waterfront terrace scene is more like an impromptu party in someone's backyard. (www.cafesoundgarden.nl; Marnixstraat 164-166; ⊗1pm-1am Mon-Thu, 1pm-3am Fri, 3pm-3am Sat, 3pm-1am Sun; 🚃13/14/17 Marnixstraat)

Tripel BEER CAFÉ

24 🚇 Map p48, B6

With affable bar staff and cosy clutter all around, Tripel feels like a real neighbourhood pub. And so it is, located off the tourist path at the Jordaan's edge. The focus is on Belgian beers: around 13 flow from the taps, with 200 more available in bottles. Reserve ahead for roasted chicken and other delicious Belgian dishes (€9.50 to 15.50) from the kitchen. (🎜370 64 21; Lijnbaansgracht 161; ⊗4pm-3am Mon-Fri, from noon Sat & Sun; 🛜; 🚃7/10/17 Elandsgracht)

🔍 Local Life
De Twee Zwaantjes

To experience the Jordaan's famous tradition of drunken singalongs, duck into **De Twee Zwaantjes** (🎜625 27 29; www.detweezwaantjes.nl; Prinsengracht 114; ⊗3pm-1am Sun-Thu, to 3am Fri & Sat; 🚃13/14/17 Westermarkt). The brown *café* is at its hilarious best on weekend nights, when you can join locals and visitors belting out classics and traditional Dutch tunes in a rollicking, unforgettable cabaret-meets-karaoke evening.

Café Tabac BAR

25 🚇 Map p48, D2

Is Café Tabac a brown *café*, a designer bar or simply an effortlessly cool place to while away a few blissful hours at the intersection of two of Amsterdam's most stunning canals? The regulars don't seem concerned about definitions, but simply enjoy the views and kicking back beneath the beamed ceilings. (www.cafetabac.eu; Brouwersgracht 101; ⊗4pm-1am Mon-Thu, to 3am Fri, 10am-3am Sat, to 1am Sun; 🛜; 🚃18/21/22 Buiten Brouwersstraat)

Café de Vergulde Gaper BROWN CAFÉ

26 🚇 Map p48, D3

Decorated with old chemists' bottles and vintage posters, this former pharmacy has amiable staff and a terrace with afternoon sun. It's popular with locals, especially for after-work drinks.

The name translates to the 'Golden Gaper', for the open-mouthed bust of a Moor traditionally posted at Dutch apothecaries. (www.deverguldegaper.nl; Prinsenstraat 30; ⊙11am-1am Sun-Thu, to 3am Fri & Sat; 🛜; 🚊13/14/17 Westermarkt)

Café Het Molenpad BAR

27 Map p48, C8

By day, this gem of a canal-side *café* is full of people poring over newspapers on the terrace. By night the atmosphere turns quietly romantic, with low lamps and candlelight illuminating little tables beneath pressed-tin ceilings. (📞625 96 80; www.cafehetmolenpad.nl; Prinsengracht 653; ⊙noon-1am Sun-Thu, to 3am Fri & Sat; 🛜; 🚊1/2/5 Prinsengracht)

Two For Joy COFFEE

28 Map p48, C1

Caffeine addicts, welcome to your new home. Two For Joy roasts its own beans and then brews them into Amsterdam's best espresso. Hang out on the vintage couches and lounge chairs, ogle the art on the exposed-brick walls, and enjoy the coffee buzz (perhaps with an egg sandwich). Two For Joy has another outlet in the Southern Canal Ring. (📞221 95 52; www.twoforjoy.nl; Haarlemmerdijk 182; ⊙7.30am-7pm Mon-Fri, 8am-6pm Sat & Sun; 🚊3 Haarlemmerplein)

La Tertulia COFFEESHOP

29 Map p48, C7

A backpackers' favourite, this mother-and-daughter-run coffeeshop has a greenhouse feel. You can sit outside by the Van Gogh–inspired murals, play some board games or contemplate the Jurassic-sized crystals by the counter. Bonus: Tertulia actually has good coffee, made with beans from a Dutch speciality roaster. (📞623 85 03; www.coffeeshoptertulia.com; Prinsen-

---

Understand
Gezelligheid

This particularly Dutch quality is one of the best reasons to visit Amsterdam. It's variously translated as snug, friendly, cosy, informal, companionable and convivial, but *gezelligheid* – the state of being *gezellig* – is something more easily experienced than defined. There's a sense of time stopping, an intimacy of the here and now that leaves all your troubles behind, at least until tomorrow. You can get the warm and fuzzy feeling in many places and situations: while nursing a brew with friends, over coffee and cake with neighbours, or lingering after a meal (the Dutch call this *natafelen*, or 'after-table-ing'). Nearly any cosy establishment lit by candles probably qualifies. Old brown *cafés*, such as 't Smalle (p56) and Café Pieper, practically have *gezelligheid* on tap.

gracht 312; ⏰11am‑7pm Tue‑Sat; 🚊7/10/17
Elandsgracht)

Saarein
GAY & LESBIAN

30 🚇 Map p48, B6

Dating from the 1600s, this one-time
feminist stronghold is still a meeting
place for lesbians, although these days
gay men are welcome too. There's a
small menu with tapas, soups and
specials. (www.saarein.info; Elandsstraat 119;
⏰4pm-1am Tue-Thu, 4pm-2am Fri, noon-2am
Sat, 2pm-1am Sun; 🚊7/10/17 Elandsgracht)

Café Pieper
BROWN CAFÉ

31 🚇 Map p48, C8

Small, unassuming and unmistak-
ably old (1665), Café Pieper features
stained-glass windows, fresh sand on
the floors, antique beer mugs hanging
from the bar and a working Belgian
beer pump (1875). Sip a Wieckse Witte
beer or a terrific cappuccino as you
marvel at the claustrophobia of the
low-ceilinged bar (after all, people were
shorter back in the 17th century – even
the Dutch). (Prinsengracht 424; ⏰noon-1am
Mon-Thu, noon-2am Fri & Sat, 2-8pm Sun;
🚊1/2/5 Prinsengracht/Leidsestraat)

Entertainment

Boom Chicago
COMEDY

32 ⭐ Map p48, B5

Boom Chicago stages seriously funny
improv-style comedy shows in English. They make fun of Dutch culture,

Felix Meritis

American culture and everything that
gets in the crosshairs. Shows take
place Wednesday through Sunday in
the main theatre. Edgier shows happen in the smaller upstairs theatre.
Saturday's late-night show is a low-
cost good time. (www.boomchicago.nl; Rozengracht 117; 🌐; 🚊13/14/17 Marnixstraat)

Felix Meritis
THEATRE

33 ⭐ Map p48, C6

Amsterdam's centre for arts, culture
and science puts on innovative
modern theatre, music and dance,
as well as talks on politics, diversity,
art, technology and literature. Its
adjoining cafe is exceptional for coffee
or cocktails by the huge windows or

outside overlooking the canal. (📞626 23 21; www.felix.meritis.nl; Keizersgracht 324; ⏰box office 9am-7pm; 📶; 🚊1/2/5 Spui)

De Nieuwe Anita
LIVE MUSIC

34 ⭐ Map p48, A5

This living-room venue expanded for noise rockers has a great *café*. Behind the bookcase-concealed door, in the back, the main room has a stage and screens cult movies on Mondays. DJs and vaudeville-type acts are also on the eclectic agenda. Entrance fees range from €3 to €7. (www.denieuweanita.nl; Frederik Hendrikstraat 111; 🚊3 Hugo de Grootplein)

Movies
CINEMA

35 ⭐ Map p48, C1

This *gezellig* art-deco cinema (the oldest in Amsterdam, dating from 1912) screens indie films alongside mainstream flicks. From Sunday to Thursday you can treat yourself to a meal in the restaurant (open 5.30pm to 10pm) or have a pre-movie tipple at its inviting *café*-bar. (📞638 60 16; www.themovies.nl; Haarlemmerdijk 161; 🚊3 Haarlemmerplein)

Maloe Melo
BLUES

36 ⭐ Map p48, B7

This is the free-wheeling, fun-loving altar of Amsterdam's tiny blues scene. Music ranges from garage and Irish punk to Texas blues and rockabilly. The cover charge is usually around €5. (📞420 45 92; www.maloemelo.com; Lijnbaansgracht 163; ⏰9pm-3am Sun-Thu, to 4am Fri & Sat; 🚊7/10/17 Elandsgracht)

Shopping

Frozen Fountain
HOMEWARES

37 🔒 Map p48, C7

The city's best-known showcase of furniture and interior design. Prices are not cheap, but the daring designs are offbeat and very memorable (designer pen-knives, kitchen gadgets and that birthday gift for the impossible-to-wow friend). Best of all, it's an unpretentious place where you can browse at length without

Café de Vergulde Gaper (p57)

feeling uncomfortable. (www.frozen
fountain.nl; Prinsengracht 645; ⏲1-6pm
Mon, 10am-6pm Tue-Sat, noon-5pm Sun;
🚊1/2/5 Prinsengracht)

Moooi Gallery   HOMEWARES

38 🔒 Map p48, C3

Founded by Marcel Wanders, this is
Dutch design at its most over-the-top,
from the life-sized black horse lamp
to the 'blow away vase' (a whimsical
twist on the classic Delft vase) and the
'killing of the piggy bank' ceramic pig
(with a gold hammer). (📞528 77 60;
www.moooi.com; Westerstraat 187; ⏲10am-
6pm Tue-Sat; 🚊3/10 Marnixplein)

Het Oud-Hollandsch Snoepwinkeltje   FOOD

39 🔒 Map p48, C4

This corner shop is lined with jar
after apothecary jar of Dutch penny
sweets with flavours from chocolate
to coffee, all manner of fruit, and the
salty Dutch liquorice known as *drop*.
It also stocks diabetic-friendly sweets.
(📞420 73 90; www.snoepwinkeltje.com;
Egelantiersdwarsstraat 2; ⏲11am-6.30pm
Tue-Sat; 🚊3/10 Marnixplein)

Back Beat Records   MUSIC

40 🔒 Map p48, C4

Back Beat has been selling jazz, soul
and funk music for close to three

decades. Whether you're looking for Sly and the Family Stone vinyl, a Chet Baker box set or a Charles Earland Hammond organ CD, this little shop has it covered. The owner is a font of local jazz lore. (📞627 16 57; www.back beat.nl; Egelantiersstraat 19; ⏱11am-6pm Mon-Sat; 🚊13/14/17 Westermarkt)

Tenue de Nîmes   CLOTHING

41 🔒 Map p48, E2

Ubercool denimwear by legendary brands such as Levi's, Rogue Territory, Pure Blue Japan, Edwin, Naked & Famous, Acne and Rag & Bone are the speciality of this hip boutique. You'll also find hot new fashions including T-shirts, stylishly cut jackets and dresses from local Amsterdam label Amatør. (www.tenuedenimes.com; Haarlemmerstraat 92-94; ⏱noon-6pm Sun & Mon, 10am-6pm Tue-Sat; 🚊18/21/22 Buiten Brouwersstraat)

I Love Vintage   VINTAGE

42 🔒 Map p48, D4

A large shop compared to most Amsterdam vintage purveyors, I Love Vintage is known for its terrific selection of dresses and jewellery from the 1920s to 1950s. It also carries retro-style new clothes if pre-worn threads aren't your thing. Prices start at around €20 and go up from there. (📞330 19 50; www.ilovevintage.com; Prinsengracht 201; ⏱9.30am-6pm Mon-Sat, noon-5pm Sun; 🚊13/14/17 Westermarkt)

De Kaaskamer   FOOD

43 🔒 Map p48, C7

The name means 'cheese room' and it is indeed stacked to the rafters with Dutch and organic varieties, as well as olives, tapenades, salads and other picnic ingredients. You can try before you

---

Understand
Dutch Design

Dutch design has a reputation for minimalist, creative approaches to every-day products, with a healthy dose of off-centre humour mixed in to keep it fresh. A few big names – such as Hella Jongerius and Marcel Wanders – are known internationally, but the best work often comes out of collectives such as Droog and Moooi.

To see Dutch design in action, check out Frozen Fountain (p60) and its tongue-in-cheek versions of Delftware and traditional textiles, as well as patchwork tables made from salvaged wood. At Droog (p138) in Nieuwmarkt, signature designs employ surreal wit, such as a chandelier made of 80-plus light bulbs clustered like fish eggs. Moooi Gallery (p61) in the Jordaan show-cases outrageous Dutch design homewares. For bargain designs, all-purpose shop Hema (p40) has developed a cult following by commissioning design students to put a spin on everything from espresso cups to handbags.

buy, and if it's too much to take home a mondo wheel of Gouda, you can at least procure a cheese and/or meat baguette to take away. (www.kaaskamer.nl; Runstraat 7; ⏰ noon-6pm Mon, 9am-6pm Tue-Fri, to 5pm Sat, noon-5pm Sun; 🚊 1/2/5 Spui)

De Kaaskamer

Galleria d'Arte Rinascimento

ART, ANTIQUES

44 🔒 Map p48, C5

This pretty shop sells Royal Delftware ceramics (both antique and new), all manner of vases, platters, brooches, Christmas ornaments and intriguing 19th-century wall tiles and plaques. (📞 622 75 09; www.delft-art-gallery.com; Prinsengracht 170; ⏰ 9am-6pm; 🚊 13/14/17 Westermarkt)

SPRMRKT

CLOTHING

45 🔒 Map p48, B6

Whether you want a supertight pair of Acne jeans, a vintage Thor Larson Pod chair or the latest copy of *Butt* magazine, it's all here at this lofty industrial concept store, a major player in Amsterdam's fashion scene. (📞 330 56 01; www.sprmrkt.nl; Rozengracht 191-193; ⏰ noon-6pm Mon, 10am-6pm Tue, Wed & Sat, 10am-7pm Thu & Fri, 1-6pm Sun; 🚊 13/14/17 Marnixstraat)

Boekie Woekie

BOOKS

46 🔒 Map p48, C6

This artist-run bookstore sells books created by artists. Some tell elegantly illustrated stories; others are riffs on graphic motifs. The merchandise is exquisitely one-of-a-kind. (www.boewoe. home.xs4all.nl; Berenstraat 16; ⏰ noon-6pm; 🚊 13/14/17 Westermarkt)

Local Life
Exploring Westerpark & Western Islands

Getting There

The area borders the Jordaan to the northwest; it's 1.6km from Centraal Station.

🚊 3 and 10 swing by the area.

🚌 22 goes to Het Schip.

A reedy wilderness, a post-industrial culture complex and a drawbridge-filled adventure await those who make the trip to Westerpark and the Western Islands. Architectural and foodie hotspots add to the hip, eco-urban mash-up. The area's rags-to-riches story is prototypical Amsterdam: abandoned factoryland hits the skids, squatters salvage it, and it rises again in creative fashion.

1 Architecture

The remarkable housing project **Het Schip** (✆418 28 85; www.hetschip.nl; Spaarndammerplantsoen 140; admission €7.50; ✆11am-5pm Tue-Sun; 🚊22 Zaanstraat) is the pinnacle of Amsterdam School architecture. Michiel de Klerk designed the triangular block, loosely resembling a ship, for railway employees. There is a small museum where you can see the old post office and an apartment.

2 Patch of Green

From Het Schip, walk southeast along the train tracks and cut through an underpass to **Westerpark** (Spaarndammerstraat & Zeeheldenbuurt; 🚊3 Haarlemmerplein). The pond-dappled green space is a cool-cat hang-out that blends into **Westergasfabriek**, a former gasworks transformed into an edgy cultural park, whose buildings hold *cafés*, theatres, breweries and other creative spaces.

3 Terrace Drinks

On sunny afternoons young, artsy professionals flock to the massive decked outdoor terrace at **Westergasterras** (www.westergasterras.nl; Klönneplein 4, Westergasfabriek; ✆11am-1am Wed & Thu, 11am-3am Fri, 10am-3am Sat, 10am-1am Sun; 🚊10 Van Limburg Stirumstraat). A toasty fireplace makes the cafe equally inviting indoors. It's perfect for a vino and mackerel salad sandwich. Late at night on weekends it morphs into a club.

4 Jazzy Notes

Respected jazz musicians (and several big names) play at welcoming **North Sea Jazz Club** (✆722 09 81; www.northseajazzclub.com; Pazzanistraat 1, Westergasfabriek; 🚊10 Van Limburg Stirumstraat). Many shows are free: up-and-coming performers let loose during 'Summer Sessions' on Wednesdays and Thursdays from 6.30pm to 9.30pm; and modern and electronic musicians play 'Late Night Live' shows on Saturdays.

5 Western Islands

The **Western Islands** (Westelijke Eilanden; 🚊48 Barentszplein) were originally home to shipworks and the West India Trading Company's warehouses, which buzzed with activity in the early 1600s. The district is a world unto itself, cut through with canals and linked with small drawbridges. It's well worth a wander among the charming homes and artist studios.

6 Scenic Zandhoek

Visit photogenic **Zandhoek** (Realeneiland; 🚊48 Barentszplein), a stretch of waterfront on the eastern shore. Now a yacht harbour, back in the 17th century it was a 'sand market', where ships would purchase bags of the stuff for ballast.

7 Foodie Love at Marius

Foodies swoon over pocket-sized **Marius** (✆422 78 80; www.deworst.nl; Barentszstraat 173; 4-course menu €47.50; ✆6.30-10pm Tue-Sat; 🚊48 Barentszplein). Chef Kees shops daily at local markets. The result might be grilled prawns with fava bean purée or beef rib with polenta and ratatouille. He also operates a sausage-and-wine bar next door.

Explore

Southern Canal Belt

Two clubby nightlife districts anchor the Southern Canal Belt: Leidseplein and Rembrandtplein. Both are neon-lit, one-stop shops for partygoers. In between lie several intriguing museums – including the art blockbuster Hermitage Amsterdam – and restaurants, cafes and shops galore. During the Golden Age, the city's wealthiest residents lived here, so add mansions on gorgeous canals to the mix, too.

The Sights in a Day

☼ Devote the morning to whatever mega art exhibit the **Hermitage Amsterdam** (p72) is showing. Then stroll over to the **Tassenmuseum Hendrikje** (p73), a museum dedicated to handbags and purses throughout history – heaven for 'ladies who lunch'.

☼ Begin the afternoon at Rembrandtplein and do the tourist thing. Snap a photo with the master painter's statue, eat a *kroket* (croquette) at **Van Dobben** (p76) and finish with a drink at splendid, velvet-chaired **De Kroon** (p78). Next saunter over to **Museum Van Loon** (p72) for a look at the moneyed canal-house life-style, and to **FOAM** (p73) for renowned photography exhibits

☾ For dinner, choose one of the smart bars and restaurants along Utrechtsestraat – maybe **Tempo Doeloe** (p76) for Indonesian and **Bar Moustache** (p78) for Italian. You'll need a solid meal to energise the evening's activities around Leidseplein. See what's on at **Paradiso** (p80), **Melkweg** (p80) and **Jazz Café Alto** (p81). Prefer something more laid-back? Try beery **Eijlders** (p78).

For a local's day in the Southern Canal Belt, see p68.

○ Local Life

Strolling the Southern Canal Belt (p68)

♥ Best of Amsterdam

Museums & Galleries
Hermitage Amsterdam (p72)

FOAM (p73)

Kattenkabinet (p69)

Tassenmuseum Hendrikje (p73)

Amsterdam Pipe Museum (p74)

Museum Van Loon (p72)

Entertainment
Melkweg (p80)

Paradiso (p80)

Jazz Café Alto (p81)

Drinking & Nightlife
Door 74 (p79)

Air (p78)

Van Dyck Bar (p79)

Getting There

🚊 **Tram** Trams 1, 2, 5, 7 and 10 go to Leidseplein. To Rembrandt-plein, take tram 4, which travels down Utrechtsestraat (bountiful for restaurants). Trams 16 and 24 cut through the centre of the neighbourhood down busy Vijzelstraat.

Local Life
Strolling the Southern Canal Belt

Puttin' on the ritz is nothing new to the Southern Canal Belt. Most of the area was built at the end of the 17th century, when Amsterdam was wallowing in Golden Age cash. A wander through reveals grand mansions, swanky antique shops, an indulgent patisserie and a one-of-a-kind kitty museum. And while it's all stately, it's certainly not snobby.

❶ Flower Market

The canal-side **Bloemenmarkt** (Flower Market; Singel, btwn Muntplein & Koningsplein; ⊙8.30am-7pm Mon-Sat, to 7.30pm Sun Apr-Oct, 9am-5.30pm Mon-Sat, 11am-5.30pm Sun Mar-Nov; 🚋1/2/5 Koningsplein) has been here since 1860. Exotic bulbs are the main stock, though cut flowers brighten the stalls, too. Buy a bouquet: there's no better way to feel like a local than walking around with flowers in the crook of your arm.

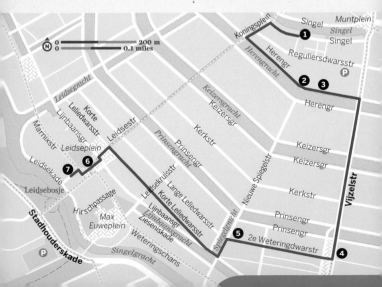

2 Golden Bend Riches

During the Golden Age, the **Golden Bend** (Gouden Bocht; Herengracht, btwn Leidsestraat & Vijzelstraat; 1/2/5 Koningsplein) was the 'it' spot, where the wealthiest Amsterdammers lived, loved and ruled their affairs. Look up at the mansions as you walk along the Herengracht. Many date from the 1660s. The gables here were allowed to be twice as wide as the standard Amsterdam model.

3 Odd Art at the Kattenkabinet

The only Golden Bend abode that's open to the public is the **Kattenkabinet** (Cats Cabinet; 626 90 40; www.kattenkabinet.nl; Herengracht 497; adult/child €7/free; 10am-5pm Mon-Fri, from noon Sat & Sun; 1/2/5 Koningsplein), an offbeat museum devoted to cat-related art. A Picasso drawing, kitschy kitty lithographs and odd pieces of ephemera cram the creaky old house. Happy live felines lounge on the window seats.

4 Treats at Patisserie Holtkamp

When you arrive at **Patisserie Holtkamp** (www.patisserieholtkamp.nl; Vijzelgracht 15; dishes €2.45-6.50; 8.30am-6pm Mon-Fri, to 5pm Sat, closed late Jul–mid-Aug; 4/7/10/16/24 Weteringcircuit), look up to spot the gilded royal coat of arms, topped by a crown, attached to the brick facade: this swanky bakery supplies the Dutch royals with delicacies including *kroketten* (croquettes) with fillings of prawns, lobster and veal.

5 Spiegel Quarter Antiques

When it's time to decorate that mansion, folks head to the long line of shops along Spiegelgracht and Nieuwe Spiegelstraat, aka the **Spiegel Quarter**. The perfect Delft vase or 16th century wall map will most assuredly be hiding among the antique stores, bric-a-brac shops and commercial art galleries.

6 Theatre Time

The neo-Renaissance **Stadsschouwburg** (624 23 11; www.stadsschouwburgamsterdam.nl; Leidseplein 26; box office noon-6pm Mon-Sat; 1/2/5/7/10 Leidseplein) takes pride of place on the Leidseplein. The regal venue, built in 1894, is used for large-scale plays, operettas and the Holland Festival, the country's biggest music, drama and arts extravaganza (held in June). Amsterdam's main ticket desk is also stashed inside, where you can get seats for shows around town.

7 Drinks at Café Americain

Pull up a chair, order a cappuccino and watch the world spin by at **Café Americain** (556 30 10; www.cafeamericain.nl; Leidsekade 97, Eden Amsterdam American Hotel; 6.30am-10.30pm; 1/2/5/7/10 Leidseplein). The art-nouveau monument, opened in 1902, was a grand *café* before the concept even existed, with huge stained-glass windows overlooking Leidseplein, a lovely, library-like reading table and a great terrace.

A B C D

1
Passeerdersgr
Molenpad
Leidsegracht
Keizersgr
Leidsegr
38
Leidsesir
Herengracht
43
16
P P
Raamstr
Lijnbaansgr
7.10
Kerkstr
15
Keizersgracht
Leidsegr
Prinsengr
Prinsengr
1.2.5
44

2
20
Lijnbaansgr
31
Marnixstr
29
Korte Lelieldwarsstr
36
Leidseplein
7 Amsterdam
Pipe Museum
Prinsengr
Prinsengracht
Nieuwe Spiegelstr
Kerkst
34
33
17

3
Leidsekade
Leidsebosje
26
Hirschpassage
Leidsekruisstr
12
18
Lijnbaansgr
Lange Lelieldwarsstr
23
45
46
Max
Euweplein
30
Zieseniskade
Weteringschans
Spiegelgr
Singelgracht
11 Prinsengr
2e Weteringdwarstr
3e Weteringdwarstr
10
Nieuwe Weteringstr
Lijnbaansgracht

4
P
Zandpad
Vossiusstr
Hobbemastr
Stadhouderskade

5
Pieter Cornelisz Hooftstr
Jan Luijkenstr
Rijksmuseum
Hobbemakade
Boerenwetering
Paulus Potterstr
2.5
N 0 200 m
0 0.1 miles

E Muntplein
F Binnen Amstel
G
H Stopera
Waterlooplein

Singel
Amstel

Singel
Korte Reguliers-
dwarsstr
Bakkerstr
Paardenstr
Wagenstr
Blauwbrug

28
eguliersdwarsstr
37 27
22
Amstelstr 21
Golden
Bend
25
Rembrandtplein
14
Museum
Willet-Holthuysen
3
1
Hermitage
Amsterdam

35
Thorbeckeplein
5
Herengr
Herengracht
Herengr
Herengr
Tassenmuseum
Hendrikje
Utrechtsestr

Vijzelstr
47
Stadsarchief
6
42
4
FOAM
Keizersgr
8
Geelvinck
Hinlopen
Huis
Reguliersgr
Keizersgr
Keizersgracht
Magere
Brug
32

2
Museum
Van Loon
Keizersgr
Keizersgr
13
40
Kerkstr

16.24
Prinsengr
Amstelveld
Utrechtsestr
Prinsengracht
Prinsengracht

9
Noorderstr
39
41
24
19
Utrechtsedwarsstr
Achtergr

Vijzelgr
Nieuwe Looiersstr
Falckstr

Fokke Simonszstr
Frederiksplein

Weteringschans
Sarphatistr

Den Texstr

Weteringcircuit
Nicolaas Witsenkade
Nicolaas Witsenstr

For reviews see
	Sights	p72
	Eating	p74
	Drinking	p78
	Entertainment	p80
	Shopping	p81

Sights

Hermitage Amsterdam
MUSEUM

1 ⊙ Map p70, H2

The long-standing ties of Russia and the Netherlands – Tsar Peter the Great learned shipbuilding here in 1697 – led to this local branch of St Petersburg's State Hermitage Museum. Blockbuster temporary exhibitions, such as treasures from the Russian palace or masterworks by Matisse and Picasso, change about twice per year, and they're as stately (and popular) as you'd expect. Come before 11am to avoid the lengthiest queues. Photography isn't permitted. (☏ 530 74 88; www.hermitage.nl; Amstel 51; adult/child €15/free; ⊙10am-5pm; Ⓜ Waterlooplein, ☐ 9/14 Waterlooplein)

☑ Top Tip

Photo Op: Reguliersgracht

It's easy to focus on the raucous nightlife and forget one of Amsterdam's most romantic canals flows through the neighbourhood. The **Reguliersgracht** (☐ 4/9/14 Rembrandtplein), aka the canal of seven bridges, is especially idyllic at night when its arched spans glow with tiny gold lights. To get the money shot, stand with your back to the Thorbeckeplein and the Herengracht flowing directly in front of you to the left and right. Lean over the bridge and look straight ahead down the Reguliersgracht. Ahhh. Now kiss your sweetie.

Museum Van Loon
MUSEUM

2 ⊙ Map p70, E3

Museum Van Loon is an opulent 1672 residence that was first home to painter Ferdinand Bol and later to the wealthy Van Loon family. The house recalls canal-side living in Amsterdam when money was no object. Inside there are important paintings such as *Wedding Portrait* by Jan Miense Molenaer and a collection of some 150 portraits of the Van Loons. (☏ 624 52 55; www.museumvanloon.nl; Keizersgracht 672; adult/child €9/5; ⊙10am-5pm; ☐ 16/24 Keizersgracht)

Museum Willet-Holthuysen
MUSEUM

3 ⊙ Map p70, G2

Built around 1685 for Amsterdam mayor Jacob Hop and redesigned in 1739, this sumptuous residence, now managed by the Amsterdam Museum, is named after the widow who bequeathed the property to the city in 1895. Highlights include paintings by Jacob de Wit, the *place de milieu* (centrepiece) that was part of the family's 275-piece Meissen table service, and the intimate French-style garden with sundial – you can also peek at the garden through the iron fence at the Amstelstraat end. (☏ 523 18 22; www.willetholthuysen.nl; Herengracht 605; adult/child €8.50/4.25; ⊙10am-5pm Mon-Fri, from 11am Sat & Sun; Ⓜ Waterlooplein, ☐ 4/9/14 Rembrandtplein)

AMYLAUGHINGHOUSE / GETTY IMAGES ©

Wooden tulips at the Bloemenmarkt (p68)

FOAM
GALLERY

4 ⊙ Map p70, E2

Simple but spacious galleries, some with skylights or grand windows for natural light, create a superb space for contemplation. The gallery features changing exhibitions spanning all genres of photography, often from world-renowned photographers such as Sir Cecil Beaton, Annie Leibovitz and Henri Cartier-Bresson. (Fotografiemuseum Amsterdam; www.foam. org; Keizersgracht 609; adult/child €10/free; ⊙10am-6pm Sat-Wed, to 9pm Thu & Fri; 🚊16/24 Keizersgracht)

Tassenmuseum Hendrikje
MUSEUM

5 ⊙ Map p70, F2

At this handbag museum you'll find half a millennium's worth of arm candy. The largest collection in the Western world (over 5000 bags), it contains everything from a crumpled 16th-century pouch to dainty art-deco and design classics by Chanel, Gucci and Versace, to Madonna's ivy-strewn 'Evita' bag from the film premiere and an '80s touch-tone phone bag. The 17th-century interiors are stunning. (Museum of Bags & Purses; 🕿524 64 52; www.tassenmuseum. nl; Herengracht 573; adult/child €12.50/7.50; ⊙10am-5pm; 🚊4/9/14 Rembrandtplein)

Stadsarchief
HISTORIC ARCHIVE

6 Map p70, E2

The Amsterdam archives occupy a monumental bank building from 1923. When you step inside, head to the left to the enormous tiled basement vault and displays of archive gems such as the 1942 police report on the theft of Anne Frank's bike. A small cinema at the back shows vintage films about the city. Tours (adult/child €6/free) run at 2pm on Saturday and Sunday and must be reserved in advance. (Municipal Archives; ☑251 15 11, tour reservations 251 15 10; www.stadsarchief.amsterdam.nl; Vijzelstraat 32; admission free; ☉10am-5pm Tue-Fri, from noon Sat & Sun; ☑16/24 Keizersgracht)

Amsterdam Pipe Museum
MUSEUM

7 Map p70, B2

Did you know that pipes were first used for smoking by Native Americans around 500 BC? It's the starting point of the history of pipes at this unexpectedly fascinating museum, which displays a private collection of objects collected over 40 years from some 60 different countries. Knowledgeable guides take you through the collection's Chinese opium pipes, Turkish water pipes, carved Maori pipes, African ceremonial pipes and much more. The opportunity to explore the beautiful 17th-century canal house is worth the admission price alone. (www.pipemuseum. nl; Prinsengracht 488; adult/child €8/4; ☉museum noon-6pm Wed-Sat, shop 11am-6pm Mon-Sat; ☑1/2/5 Prinsengracht)

Geelvinck Hinlopen Huis
MUSEUM

8 Map p70, F2

To see how the wealthy lived during the 17th century, visit this 1687-built private mansion and its magnificent classical gardens linking the former Keizersgracht coach house with the main Herengracht house, and incorporating a herb garden, English garden and French formal garden with Amsterdam's largest private pond. English-speaking guides are on hand to show you the mansion's rooms. Concerts, many using the estate's vintage instruments, take place on Sundays at 4.45pm (tickets per adult/child from €18/12). (☑639 07 47; www.geelvinck.nl; Keizersgracht 633; adult/child €9/4.50; ☉11am-5pm Wed-Mon; ☑16/24 Keizersgracht)

Eating

Restaurant Fyra
MODERN EUROPEAN €€€

9 Map p70, E4

Many of the vegetables and herbs at this local foodies' favourite are grown in the owner-chef's garden and used in stunning creations like pea and mint soup with local prawns; barbecued tenderloin with potato mousseline; and marinated peaches with Dutch yoghurt, meringue and pomegranate syrup. There's a wonderful selection of cheeses and wines. (☑428 36 32; www.restaurant fyra.nl; Noorderstraat 19-23; 3-/4-/5-/6-course menus €36/42.50/47.50/52.50; ☉6-11pm; ☑16/24 Weteringcircuit)

La Cacerola

BRAZILIAN €€

10 🍴 Map p70, D4

At this rustic, romantic gem, dishes prepared according to traditional methods and Slow Food principles include wild sea bass marinated in lime juice; spiced rack of milk-fed lamb; and house-speciality *churrasco de picanha* (steak barbecued on a charcoal grill and served with spicy pumpkin purée). If you can't decide, go for the chef's surprise four-course menu (€34.50). Service is superb. (📞 627 93 97; www.restaurantlacacerola.nl; Weteringstraat 41; mains €21.50-24.50; ⏱ 6-10.30pm Tue-Sat; 🚊 7/10 Spiegelgracht)

Buffet van Odette

CAFE €€

11 🍴 Map p70, D3

Not a buffet but an airy, white-tiled, sit-down cafe with a beautiful canal-side terrace, where Odette shows how good simple cooking can taste when you start with great ingredients and a dash of creativity. Soups, sandwiches, pastas and quiches are mostly organic with smart little extras like pine nuts or truffle cheese. (📞 423 60 34; www.buffetvanodette.nl; Prinsengracht 598; mains lunch €8-15.50, dinner €15.50-19; ⏱ kitchen 10am-10pm; 🍴; 🚊 7/10 Spiegelgracht)

Pantry

DUTCH €€

12 🍴 Map p70, B3

Wood-panelled walls and sepia lighting make this *gezellig* (cosy, convivial) little restaurant an atmospheric place for classic Dutch cooking: *haring met uitjes en zuur* (salted herring with onions and pickles); *zuurkool stamppot* (sauerkraut and potato mash served with a smoked sausage or meatball); *hutspot* ('hotchpotch', with stewed beef, carrots and onions); and *stroopwafelijs* (caramel-syrup-filled, wafer-like waffles, with ice cream). (📞 620 09 22; thepantry.nl; Leidsekruisstraat 21; mains €13-18, 3-course menus €20-28; ⏱ 11am-10.30pm; 🍴; 🚊 1/2/5 Leidseplein)

Understand
How to Eat a Herring

'Hollandse Nieuwe' isn't a fashion trend – it's the fresh catch of super-tasty herring raked in every June. The Dutch love it, and you'll see vendors selling the salty fish all over town. Although Dutch tradition calls for dangling the herring above your mouth, this isn't the way it's done in Amsterdam. Here the fish is served chopped in chunks, and eaten with a toothpick, topped with *uitjes* (chopped onions) and *zuur* (sweet pickles). A *broodje haring* (herring roll) is even handier, as the fluffy white roll holds on the toppings and keeps your fingers free of fish fat – think of it as an edible napkin.

Tempo Doeloe INDONESIAN €€€

13 Map p70, G3

Consistently ranked among Amsterdam's finest Indonesian restaurants, Tempo Doeloe's setting and service are elegant without being overdone. The same applies to the *rijsttafel* (literally 'rice table'): a ridiculously overblown affair at many places, here it's a fine sampling of the range of dishes found in the country. Warning: dishes marked 'very hot' are indeed like napalm. The wine list is excellent. (☑625 67 18; www.tempodoeloerestaurant.nl; Utrechtsestraat 75; mains €23.50-38.50, rijsttafel & set menus €29-49; ☺6-11.30pm Mon-Sat; ☑; ☐4 Prinsengracht)

Van Dobben DUTCH €

14 Map p70, F1

Open since the 1940s, Van Dobben has white-tile walls and white-coated staff who specialise in snappy banter. Traditional meaty Dutch fare is its forte: try the *pekelvlees* (something close to corned beef), or make it a *halfom* (if you're keen on that being mixed with liver). (☑624 42 00; www.eetsalonvandobben.nl; Korte Reguliersdwarsstraat 5-9; dishes €2.75-8; ☺10am-9pm Mon-Wed, 10am-1am Thu, 10am-2am Fri & Sat, 10.30am-8pm Sun; ☐4/9/14 Rembrandtplein)

Ron Gastrobar Oriental ASIAN €€

15 Map p70, B1

Ron Blaauw revolutionised dining at Ron Gastrobar (p98) near Vondelpark when he traded his Michelin stars for a one-price menu of tapas-style dishes, and he's recreated the red-hot concept here, this time with an Asian focus. Small plates include dim sum with foie gras, poached chicken with peanut sauce, Wagyu steak tartare, Oriental spare ribs, crispy prawns, and roast Peking duck. (☑223 53 52; www.rongastrobaroriental.nl; Kerkstraat 23; dishes €15; ☺5.30-11pm; ☎; ☐1/2/5 Prinsengracht)

Bar Huf AMERICAN €

16 Map p70, D1

You can just drop by for a beer/cocktail but Bar Huf really comes into its own for late-night dining. Five different burgers (Mango Jerry: crab, coleslaw and wasabi mayo; Rocky Balboa: chicken, jalapeños and cheddar), rum- and apple-glazed ribs, macaroni and cheese (made with five different cheeses), and lemon meringue pie are

---

○ Local Life
Piet de Leeuw

A steakhouse and hang-out since the 1940s, **Piet de Leeuw** (☑623 71 81; www.pietdeleeuw.nl; Noorderstraat 11; mains €12.50-21.50; ☺noon-10.30pm Mon-Fri, from 5pm Sat & Sun; ☐16/24 Keizersgracht) has a dark and cosy atmosphere that has barely changed since. If you don't get your own table, you may make friends at a common table. Good-value beef slabs are served with piping-hot *frites* (French fries).

De Kroon (p78)

all available long after nearby restaurants have closed. (barhuf.nl; Reguliersdwarsstraat 43; mains €8.50-14.50; ⊙kitchen 4pm midnight Sun Thu, to 1am Fri & Sat; 🛜; 🚊1/2/5 Koningsplein)

Lavinia Good Food   VEGETARIAN €
17 🍴 Map p70, D3

Spelt minipizzas, portobello mushroom burgers, salads like pasta or chickpea, and sandwiches with toppings like mango salsa, hummus and guacamole make Lavinia a delicious stop even if you're not vegetarian. (www.laviniagoodfood.nl; Kerkstraat 176; dishes €4.50-8.50; ⊙8.30am-4pm Mon-Fri, 9.30am-5pm Sat & Sun; 🖊; 🚊16/24 Keizersgracht)

In de Buurt   INTERNATIONAL €€
18 🍴 Map p70, B3

A canal-side summer terrace and interior of exposed brick walls and stainless-steel downlights provide a relaxed backdrop for fantastic miniburgers with truffle mayo and roasted cherry tomatoes, cannelloni stuffed with Dutch goat's cheese and spinach, and grilled whole sea bream with tarragon oil, but the star of the show is the homemade chocolate and pecan brownie with white-chocolate sauce. (www.inderbuurt-amsterdam.nl; Lijnbaansgracht 246; mains €14.50-20.50; ⊙kitchen 5-10pm Mon-Thu, from 3pm Fri, from 2pm Sat & Sun; 🚊1/2/5 Leidseplein)

Drinking

Bar Moustache
BAR

19 Map p70, G4

With an exposed-brick, minimalist interior designed by Stella Willing, this loft-style cafe-bar has a mix of communal and private tables that fill with hip locals, and a couple of coveted windowsill benches to watch the action along Utrechtsestraat. There's a stunning, pared-down Italian menu and a great drink selection including Italian wines by the glass. (www.barmoustache.nl; Utrechtsestraat 141; ⊙8am-1am Mon-Thu, 8am-3am Fri, 9am-3am Sat, 9am-1am Sun; 🚊4 Prinsengracht)

Eijlders
BROWN CAFÉ

20 Map p70, A2

During WWII, this beautiful stained-glass brown *café* (pub) was a meeting place for artists who refused to toe the cultural line imposed by the Nazis, and the spirit lingers on. It's still an artists' cafe, hosting regular poetry readings (sometimes in English – call to be sure), jam sessions and exhibitions. (www.cafeeijlders.nl; Korte Leliedwarsstraat 47; ⊙4.30pm-1am Mon-Wed, noon-1am Thu & Sun, noon-2am Fri & Sat; 🚊1/2/5/7/10 Leidseplein)

Air
CLUB

21 Map p70, G1

One of Amsterdam's 'it' clubs, Air has an environmentally friendly design by Dutch designer Marcel Wanders including a unique tiered dance floor. Bonuses include lockers and refillable cards that preclude fussing with change at the five bars. The awesome sound system attracts cutting-edge DJs spinning everything from disco to house and techno to hip hop. Hours vary; dress to impress. (www.air.nl; Amstelstraat 16; ⊙Thu-Sun; 🚊4/9/14 Rembrandtplein)

De Kroon
GRAND CAFÉ

22 Map p70, F1

Restored to its 1898 splendour, De Kroon has high ceilings, velvet chairs, and a beautiful art-deco tiled staircase up the two floors above Rembrandtplein (there's also a lift). Sit at the atmospheric English-library-themed bar and be mesmerised by the curious display of 19th-century medical equipment. (www.dekroon.nl; Rembrandtplein 17; ⊙4pm-1am Mon-Thu, 4pm-4am Fri, 11am-4am Sat, 11am-1am Sun; 🚊4/9/14 Rembrandtplein)

Sweet Cup
COFFEE

23 Map p70, C3

Run by a fun-loving young Dutch couple, this aromatic microroastery supplies coffee to many local cafes, but you can drink it here at the source or pick up a cup to take away, with a choice of five espresso styles and five slow brews. It also sells roasted beans. (www.sweetcupcafe.com; Lange Leliedwarsstraat 101; ⊙8am-6pm Mon & Wed-Fri, 9am-6pm Sat, 11am-6pm Sun; 🚊1/2/5 Leidseplein)

Pata Negra
WINE BAR

24 Map p70, G4

The freshly squeezed margaritas are tops at this Spanish tapas bar. Its rustic tiled exterior is matched by a vibrant crowd inside, especially on weekends, downing sangria with garlic-fried shrimps and grilled sardines (tapas cost €4.50 to €10). It gets packed, and that's half the fun. (www.pata-negra.nl; Utrechtsestraat 124; ⏱noon-1am Sun-Thu, to 3am Fri & Sat; 🚋4 Prinsengracht)

Door 74
COCKTAIL BAR

25 🚇 Map p70, E1

You'll need to leave a voice message or, better yet, send a text for a reservation to gain entry to this cocktail bar behind an unmarked door. Some of Amsterdam's most amazing cocktails are served in a classy, dark-timbered speakeasy atmosphere beneath pressed-tin ceilings. Themed cocktail lists change regularly. Very cool. (📞06 3404 5122; www.door-74.nl; Reguliersdwarsstraat 74; ⏱8pm-3am Sun-Thu, to 4am Fri & Sat; 🚋9/14 Rembrandtplein)

Van Dyck Bar
CLUB

26 🚇 Map p70, B3

Van Dyck brings Ibiza-style clubbing to Amsterdam, with wicked lighting and sound systems and DJs who know how to pack the dance floor. There's usually no cover before midnight; dress up to get past the door. (www. vandyckbar.com; Korte Leliedwarsstraat 28-32; ⏱10pm-4am Wed, Thu & Sun, to 5am Fri & Sat; 🚋1/2/5/7/10 Leidseplein)

⊙ Local Life
Utrechtsestraat
A stone's throw south from gaudy Rembrandtplein, **Utrechtsestraat** is a relaxed artery stocked with enticing shops, designer bars and cosy eateries – a prime place to wander and discover a great local hang-out. The street's southern end used to terminate at the Utrechtse Poort, a gate to the nearby city of Utrecht, hence the name.

Montmartre
GAY BAR

27 🚇 Map p70, F1

Regarded by many as the best gay bar in Benelux, and a busy weekend will show why. Patrons sing along (or scream along) to recordings of Dutch ballads and old top-40 hits. (www.cafemontmartre.nl; Halvemaansteeg 17; ⏱5pm-1am Sun-Thu, to 4am Fri & Sat, 🚋4/9/14 Rembrandtplein)

Taboo Bar
GAY BAR

28 🚇 Map p70, E1

Taboo's wicked two-for-one happy hours (6pm to 7pm and midnight to 1am, plus 6pm to 8pm Sunday) guarantee a good time. Wednesday is cocktail night, when cocktails cost just €6 and a drag show and competitions like 'pin the tail on the sailor' take place. (www. taboobar.nl; Reguliersdwarsstraat 45; ⏱5pm-3am Mon-Thu, 5pm-4am Fri, 4pm-4am Sat, 4pm-3am Sun; 🛜; 🚋1/2/5 Koningsplein)

Entertainment

Melkweg
LIVE MUSIC

29 ⭐ Map p70, A2

In a former dairy, the nonprofit 'Milky Way' is a dazzling galaxy of diverse music. One night it's electronica, the next reggae or punk, and the next heavy metal. Roots, rock and mellow singer-songwriters all get stage time too. Check out the website for cutting-edge cinema, theatre and multimedia offerings. (www.melkweg.nl; Lijnbaansgracht 234a; ◷6pm-1am; 🚊1/2/5/7/10 Leidseplein)

Paradiso
LIVE MUSIC

30 ⭐ Map p70, B3

This historic club in a gorgeous old church opened in 1968 as 'Cosmic Relaxation Center Paradiso'. Midweek club nights have low cover charges;

✅ Top Tip

Discount Tickets

Not sure how to spend your evening? Head to the **Last Minute Ticket Shop** (📞624 23 11; www.lastminuteticketshop.nl; Leidseplein 26; ◷shop noon-6pm, online ticket sales from 10am; 🚊1/2/5/7/10 Leidseplein), on the terrace side of the Stadsschouwburg on the Leidseplein. Same-day tickets to just about anything – comedy, dance, concerts – are available for half-price. Shows are handily marked 'LNP' (language no problem) if understanding Dutch isn't vital.

---

the Small Hall upstairs is an intimate venue for up-and-coming bands. The real attraction, of course, is hearing artists like the White Stripes and Lady Gaga rock the Main Hall, wondering if the stained-glass windows might shatter. (📞622 45 21; www.paradiso.nl; Weteringschans 6; ◷hours vary; 🚊1/2/5/7/10 Leidseplein)

Sugar Factory
LIVE MUSIC

31 ⭐ Map p70, A2

The vibe at this self-described 'cutting-edge multidisciplinary night theatre' is always welcoming and creative. It's definitely not your average club – most nights start with music, cinema, dance or a spoken-word performance, followed by late-night DJs and dancing. Sunday's Wicked Jazz Sounds party is a sweet one, bringing DJs, musicians, singers and actors together to improvise. (www.sugarfactory.nl; Lijnbaansgracht 238; ◷6pm-5am; 🚊1/2/5/7/10 Leidseplein)

Koninklijk Theater Carré
PERFORMING ARTS

32 ⭐ Map p70, H3

This esteemed theatre was built in 1887 by the Carré family, who'd started their career with a horse act at the annual fair. The classical facade is richly decorated with faces of jesters, dancers and theatre folk. It hosts high-calibre musicals, theatre and dance events; its Christmas circus is a seasonal highlight. Saturday-morning tours are in English and Dutch. (📞524 94 52; carre.nl; Amstel 115-125; tour adult/

child €9.50/6.50; ⊙box office 9am-9pm
Mon-Fri, 10am-8pm Sat & Sun, one-hour tour
11am Sat; Ⓜ Weesperplein)

Jazz Café Alto   JAZZ

33 ⭐ Map p70, B3

Serious jazz and blues play at this
respected cafe near Leidseplein.
Doors open at 9pm but music starts
around 10pm – get here early if you
want to snag a seat. (www.jazz-cafe-alto.
nl; Korte Leidsedwarsstraat 115; ⊙from 9pm;
🚋1/2/5/7/10 Leidseplein)

Bourbon Street
Jazz & Blues Club   JAZZ, BLUES

34 ⭐ Map p70, B3

Catch blues, funk, soul and rock and
roll in this intimate venue, with open
jam sessions on Mondays when everyone's welcome to take part. Tuesday
is soul and reggae, Wednesday blues
and rock, Thurday soul and funk,
Friday rock, pop and Latin, Saturday
pre-rock, and Sunday world, folk and
samba. Entry's free before 11pm, when
most concerts start. (www.bourbonstreet.
nl; Leidsekruisstraat 6-8; ⊙10pm-4am Sun-
Thu, to 5am Fri & Sat; 🚋1/2/5 Prinsengracht)

De Heeren van Aemstel LIVE MUSIC

35 ⭐ Map p70, F2

Students in particular cram into this
grand-café-style club to enjoy the roster of live big bands and pop and rock
cover bands. (www.deheerenvanaemstel.nl;
Thorbeckeplein 5; ⊙noon-3am Mon-Thu, to
4am Fri & Sat; 🚋4/9/14 Rembrandtplein)

Cave   LIVE MUSIC

36 ⭐ Map p70, B2

One for purists, this underground
venue (in all senses; it's buried in a
basement, hence its name) hosts live
hard-rock and metal gigs Thursday to
Saturday, and has DJs spinning the
same the rest of the week. (☎626 89 39;
www.thecave.nl; Prinsengracht 472; live music
tickets from €5; ⊙8pm-3am Sun-Thu, to 4am
Fri & Sat; 🚋1/2/5 Prinsengracht)

Pathé Tuschinskitheater   CINEMA

37 ⭐ Map p70, F1

Amsterdam's most famous cinema is
worth visiting for its sumptuous art-
deco/Amsterdam School interior alone.
The *grote zaal* (main auditorium) is the
most stunning and generally screens
blockbusters; the smaller theatres play
art-house and indie films. (www.pathe.
nl; Reguliersbreestraat 26-34; ⊙11.30am-
12.30am; 🚋4/9/14 Rembrandtplein)

Shopping

Young Designers United CLOTHING

38 🔒 Map p70, C1

Racks are rotated regularly at this
affordable women's clothing boutique
showcasing young designers working
in the Netherlands. You might spot
durable basics by Agna K; hand-
made leggings by Leg-Inc; geometric
dresses by Fenny Faber; and 'punk
rock grunge meets fairytale romance'
fashion by Jutka en Riska. Accessorise

with YDU's select range of jewellery and bags. (YDU; www.ydu.nl; Keizersgracht 447; ⊙1-6pm Mon, 10am-6pm Tue, Wed, Fri & Sat, 10am-8pm Thu; 🚊1/2/5 Keizersgracht)

MaisonNL HOMEWARES, CLOTHING

39 🔒 Map p70, G4

This gorgeous little concept store looks like a cross between an art gallery and someone's stylish apartment. Artfully displayed products range from tea sets to baby shoes, lamps to shawls, jewellery to leather handbags; there's also a clothing rack. (www.maisonnl.com; Utrechtsestraat 118; ⊙1-6pm Mon, 10.30am-6pm Tue-Sat, 1-5pm Sun; 🚊4 Prinsengracht)

Mobilia HOMEWARES

40 🔒 Map p70, G3

Dutch and international design is stunningly showcased at this three-storey 'lifestyle studio': sofas, workstations, bookshelves, lighting, cushions, rugs and much more from both emerging and established designers. (www.mobilia.nl; Utrechtsestraat 62; ⊙9.30am-6pm Mon-Sat; 🚊4 Prinsengracht)

Centre Neuf CLOTHING

41 🔒 Map p70, G4

Centre Neuf is a favourite with fashion-savvy locals for to-die-for pieces from IRO, Pomandère, YMC, Marc by Marc Jacobs, Athé by Vanessa Bruno, Aaiko, Dante 6 and Avril Gau. Luscious handbags and shoes too. (centreneuf.com; Utrechtsestraat 120; ⊙1-6pm Mon, 10am-6pm Tue-Sat, 1-5pm Sun; 🚊4 Prinsengracht)

Skateboards Amsterdam SPORTS

42 🔒 Map p70, E2

Local skater dudes and dudettes shop for cruisers, longboards, shoes, clothing including Spitfire and Skate Mental T-shirts, caps, bags and backpacks, books and music at this independent boutique. (skateboardsamsterdam.nl; Vijzelstraat 77; ⊙1-6pm Sun & Mon, 11am-6pm Tue, Wed, Fri & Sat, 11am-8pm Thu; 🚊16/24 Keizersgracht)

Marañon Hangmatten OUTDOORS

43 🔒 Map p70, D1

Anyone who loves hanging around should come and explore Europe's largest selection of hammocks. The colourful creations, made of everything from cotton to pineapple fibres, are made by many producers, from indigenous weavers to large manufacturers. It ships worldwide. (www.maranon.net; Singel 488; ⊙10.30am-5.15pm Mon-Fri, 10am-5.30pm Sat, 10.30am-5pm Sun; 🚊1/2/5 Koningsplein)

Cora Kemperman CLOTHING

44 🔒 Map p70, B2

Kemperman was once a designer with large Dutch fashion houses, but since 1995 she's been working on her own empire – now encompassing nine stores, including three in Belgium. Her well-priced creations feature mainly solid colours, floaty, layered separates and dresses in linen, cotton and wool. (📞625 12 84; www.corakemperman.nl; Leidsestraat 72; ⊙noon-6pm Sun & Mon, 10am-6pm Tue, Wed, Fri & Sat, 10am-9pm Thu; 🚊1/2/5 Prinsengracht)

JAMIE CARSTAIRS / ALAMY PHOTO STOCK ©

Eduard Kramer

Tinkerbell
CHILDREN

45 Map p70, C3

The mechanical bear blowing bubbles outside this shop fascinates kids, as do the intriguing technical and scientific toys inside. You'll also find historical costumes, plush toys and a section for babies. (www.tinkerbelltoys.nl; Spiegelgracht 10; ⏱1-6pm Mon, 10am-6pm Tue-Sat, noon-5pm Sun; 🚊7/10 Spiegelgracht)

Eduard Kramer
ANTIQUES

46 Map p70, D3

Specialising in antique Dutch tiles, this tiny store is also crammed with lots of other interesting stuff – silver candlesticks, crystal decanters, jewellery and pocket watches. (www.antique-tileshop.nl; Prinsengracht 807; ⏱11am-6pm Mon, 10am-6pm Tue-Sat, 1-6pm Sun; 🚊7/10 Spiegelgracht)

Stadsboekwinkel
BOOKS

47 Map p70, E2

Run by the city printer, this is the best source for books about Amsterdam's history, urban development, ecology and politics. Most titles are in Dutch (if you don't read it, you can always look at the pictures), but you'll also find some in English. It's in the Stadsarchief (p74) archives building. (www.stadsboekwinkel.nl; Vijzelstraat 32; ⏱10am-5pm Tue-Fri, from noon Sat & Sun; 🚊16/24 Keizersgracht)

Explore

Vondelpark & Old South

Often called the Museum Quarter, the Old South holds the top-draw Van Gogh, Stedelijk and Rijksmuseum collections. It's one of Amsterdam's richest neighbourhoods, and impressive manors rise along leafy streets. Vondelpark is the city's bucolic playground next door, where joggers, picnickers, dope smokers, accordion players and frolicking children all cheerfully coexist.

The Sights in a Day

☀️ Take a spin around beloved **Vondelpark** (p94). Long and thin – about 1.5km long and 300m wide – it's easy to explore via a morning jaunt. **Het Groot Melkhuis** (p102) and other eateries in the park offer sustenance. You'll see a cross section of freewheeling Amsterdam life hanging out here.

☼ Pay homage to the arts in the afternoon (when crowds are lighter). Fortify with a meaty lunch at **l'Entrecôte et les Dames** (p99) in the Old South, then hit the trail around the Museumplein. You'll likely have the stamina for just the **Van Gogh Museum** (p86) and **Rijksmuseum** (p90), but kudos if you fit in the modern **Stedelijk Museum** (p97) as well. They're all lined up in a walkable row.

🌙 The streets around Overtoom and Amstelveenseweg burst with stylish eateries. For dinner go for hip Dutch tapas at **Ron Gastrobar** (p98) or chic gastronomy at **Adam** (p99). Afterwards get cultured under the stars at Vondelpark's free **Openluchttheater** (p102), or listen to classical music soar in the pristine acoustics of the **Concertgebouw** (p102).

👁 Top Sights

Van Gogh Museum (p86)

Rijksmuseum (p90)

Vondelpark (p94)

❤️ Best of Amsterdam

Museums & Galleries
Stedelijk Museum (p97)

Eating
Ron Gastrobar (p98)

Restaurant Blauw (p100)

Braai BBQ Bar (p99)

Entertainment
Concertgebouw (p102)

OCCII (p102)

Drinking & Nightlife
Franklin (p100)

Shopping
Museum Shop at the Museumplein (p103)

Getting There

🚃 **Tram** Trams 2 and 5 run from the city centre and stop at the Museumplein's venues and at the main entrance to Vondelpark. Tram 1 reaches attractions deeper within Vondelpark and the bars and restaurants along Overtoom.

Top Sights
Van Gogh Museum

The world's largest Van Gogh collection is a superb line-up of masterworks. Opened in 1973 to house the collection of Vincent's art-dealer brother, Theo, the museum comprises some 200 paintings and 500 drawings by Vincent and his contemporaries, including Gauguin and Monet. Chart Van Gogh's evolution from depicting sombre countryfolk in the Netherlands to his giddy, colour-swirled landscapes in France.

👁 Map p96, D3

📞 570 52 00

www.vangoghmuseum.nl

Paulus Potterstraat 7

adult/child €17/free

🕙 9am-6pm Sun-Thu, to 10pm Fri & Sat

🚊 2/3/5/12 Van Baerlestraat

Van Gogh Museum

Don't Miss

Entrance & Set-Up

A dazzling new glass entrance hall opened in 2015, adding 800 sq metres of additional space. The museum spreads over four levels, from Floor 0 (aka the ground floor) to Floor 3. The paintings tend to be moved around, depending on the current exhibition theme (say, Van Gogh's images of nature). Seminal works to look for are listed below.

Potato Eaters

Van Gogh's earliest works – shadowy and crude – are from his time in the Dutch countryside and in Antwerp between 1883 and 1885. He was particularly obsessed with peasants – *The Potato Eaters* (1885) is his most famous painting from this period.

Bible & Skeleton

Still Life with Bible (1885) is another early work, and it shows his religious inclination. The burnt-out candle is said to represent the recent death of his father, who was a Protestant minister. *Skeleton with Burning Cigarette* (1886) was painted when Van Gogh was a student at Antwerp's Royal Academy of Fine Arts.

Self-Portraits

In 1886 Van Gogh moved to Paris, where his brother, Theo, was working as an art dealer. Vincent wanted to master the art of portraiture, but was too poor to pay for models. Several self-portraits resulted. You can see his palette begin to brighten as he comes under the influence of the Impressionists in the city.

☑ Top Tips

▶ Entrance queues can be long. Try waiting until after 3pm.

▶ Discount cards and prebooked tickets expedite the process. I Amsterdam Card holders have a separate 'fast' lane for entry. E-ticket holders also get in more quickly.

▶ E-tickets are available online or at tourist offices, with no surcharge. They must be printed.

▶ Visit on Friday evenings, when the museum stays open late, serves drinks and hosts special cultural events.

✗ Take a Break

Grab a table by the museum café's big windows, and nibble on quiche and wine while overlooking the grassy Museumplein. The eatery is open during museum hours. Or walk a few blocks to l'Entrecôte et les Dames (p99) for desserts in its gorgeous room.

Sunflowers

In 1888 Van Gogh left for Arles in Provence to delve into its landscapes. *Sunflowers* (1889) and other blossoms that shimmer with intense Mediterranean light are from this period.

The Yellow House & Bedroom

Other paintings from his time in Arles include *The Yellow House* (1888), a rendering of the abode Van Gogh rented in town, intending to start an artists' colony with Gauguin. *The Bedroom* (1888) depicts Van Gogh's sleeping quarters at the house. It was in 1888 that Van Gogh sliced off part of his ear.

Wheatfield with Crows

Van Gogh had himself committed to an asylum in St Remy in 1889. While there he painted several landscapes with cypress and olive trees, and went wild with *Irises*. In 1890 he went north to Auvers-sur-Oise. *Wheatfield with Crows* (1890), one of his last paintings, is an ominous work finished shortly before his suicide.

Sketchbooks & Letters

Intriguing displays enhance what's on the walls. For instance, you might see Van Gogh's actual sketchbook alongside an interactive kiosk that lets you page through a reproduction of it. The museum has categorised all of Van Gogh's letters online at www.vangoghletters.org. Use the museum's free wi-fi to access them with your smartphone.

Other Artists

Thanks to Theo van Gogh's prescient collecting and that of the museum's curators, you'll also see works by Vincent's contemporaries, including Gauguin, Monet and Henri de Toulouse-Lautrec.

Exhibition Wing

Gerrit Rietveld, the influential Dutch architect, designed the museum's main building. Behind it, reaching toward the Museumplein, is a separate wing (opened in 1999) designed by Kisho Kurokawa and commonly referred to as 'the Mussel'. It hosts temporary exhibitions by big-name artists.

Understand
Rich Afterlife

While Van Gogh would come to be regarded as a giant among artists, he sold only one painting during his lifetime (*Red Vineyard at Arles*, in case you're wondering; it hangs at Moscow's Pushkin Museum). Fame didn't arrive until a few decades after his death, and Van Gogh has his sister-in-law Johanna (Theo's wife) to thank for it. Johanna came from a wealthy Amsterdam family and used her connections to promote Vincent's work. She did a heck of a job – his *Portrait of Dr Gachet* (US$82 million) and *Irises* (US$54 million) are among the most expensive paintings ever sold. It's a far cry from the 400 francs (US$1600) he earned on his lone paycheck for a canvas.

Van Gogh Museum

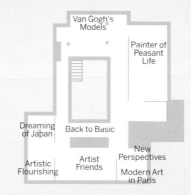

Van Gogh's Models

Painter of Peasant Life

Dreaming of Japan

Back to Basic

Artistic Flourishing

Artist Friends

New Perspectives

Modern Art in Paris

Floor 1

Self-Portraits

Cafe

Timeline

Group Entrance

Paulus Potterstraat

To Main Entrance & Exhibition Wing

Shop

Floor 0

Top Sights
Rijksmuseum

The Rijksmuseum is the Netherlands' premier art trove, and no self-respecting visitor to Amsterdam can afford to miss it. The museum was conceived as a repository for several national collections, including art owned by the royal family. Today, Rembrandts, Vermeers, porcelains and countless other treasures spill out of its 1.5km of gallery space, which incorporates 80 separate galleries. You can see the highlights in a couple of hours, but art buffs will want to allocate longer.

National Museum

◉ Map p96, E2

☏ 674 70 00

www.rijksmuseum.nl

Museumstraat 1

adult/child €17.50/free

🕓 9am-5pm

🚋 2/5 Rijksmuseum

Rijksmuseum

Don't Miss

Floor 2: Golden Age Masterpieces

The museum's top draws are in the Gallery of Honour on Floor 2. After you go through the ticket gate, head right past the audio-tour desk and go up the stairs (the ones by the sign marked 'The Collection'). Walk back to the next set of stairs and ascend – you're following the '1600–1700' signs. Eventually you'll come to the Great Hall. Push open the glass doors and behold the Golden Age's greatest works.

Frans Hals

The first room displays several paintings by Frans Hals, who painted with broad brushstrokes and a fluidity that was unique for the time. *The Merry Drinker* (1628–30) shows his style in action. No one knows who the gent with the beer glass is, but it's clear he's enjoying himself after a hard day of work.

Johannes (Jan) Vermeer

The next room holds popular Vermeer works. Check out the dreamy *Kitchen Maid* (1660) for Vermeer's famed attention to detail. See the holes in the wall? The nail with shadow? In *Woman in Blue Reading a Letter* (1663) Vermeer uses a different style. He shows only parts of objects, such as the tables and chairs, leaving the viewer to figure out the rest.

Jan Steen

Another Jan hangs across the hall from Vermeer. Jan Steen became renowned for painting chaotic households, such as the one in *The Merry Family* (1668). Everyone is having such a good time in the picture, no one notices the little boy sneaking a taste of wine.

☑ Top Tips

▶ Entrance queues can be long. Try waiting until after 3pm.

▶ Buy and print your ticket online to save time. There's no surcharge. While you still must wait in the outdoor queue, once inside you can proceed straight into the museum (otherwise you must stand in another queue to pay).

▶ Download the museum's free app (there's wi-fi on-site). It offers seven tours through the collection.

✗ Take a Break

Snack on pastries, sandwiches, coffee and beer at the mod Rijksmuseum Café (open 9am to 6pm) in the sky-lit atrium. Or head outside where snack vendors line the sidewalk between the Rijks and Van Gogh museums, serving sandwiches, pancakes, ice cream and drinks you can take to the vendors' outdoor tables.

Rijksmuseum

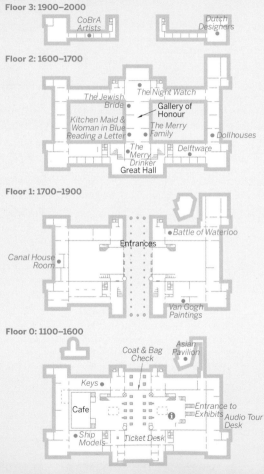

Floor 3: 1900–2000

CoBrA Artists

Dutch Designers

Floor 2: 1600–1700

The Jewish Bride

The Night Watch

Gallery of Honour

Kitchen Maid & Woman in Blue Reading a Letter

The Merry Family

Dollhouses

The Merry Drinker

Delftware

Great Hall

Floor 1: 1700–1900

Battle of Waterloo

Entrances

Canal House Room

Van Gogh Paintings

Floor 0: 1100–1600

Coat & Bag Check

Asian Pavilion

Keys

Cafe

Entrance to Exhibits

Audio Tour Desk

Ship Models

Ticket Desk

Rembrandt

You'll pass through a room of landscape paintings, and then come to a gallery of Rembrandt's works. *The Jewish Bride* (1665), showing a couple's intimate caress, impressed Van Gogh.

Night Watch

Rembrandt's gigantic *Night Watch* (1642) takes pride of place in the room. It shows the militia led by Frans Banning Cocq. The work is actually titled *Archers under the Command of Captain Frans Banning Cocq*. The Night Watch name was bestowed years later, thanks to a layer of grime that gave the impression it was evening. It's since been restored to its original colours.

Delftware

Intriguing Golden Age swag fills the rooms on either side of the Gallery of Honour. Delftware was the Dutch attempt to reproduce Chinese porcelain in the late 1600s. Gallery 2.22 displays scads of the delicate blue-and-white pottery.

Dollhouses

Gallery 2.20 is devoted to mind-blowing dollhouses. Merchant's wife Petronella Oortman employed carpenters, glassblowers and silversmiths to make the 700 items inside her dollhouse, using the same materials as they would for full-scale versions.

Floor 3: 1900–2000

The uppermost floor holds a fairly limited collection. It includes avant-garde, childlike paintings by Karel Appel, Constant Nieuwenhuys and their CoBrA compadres (a post-WWII movement) and cool furnishings by Dutch designers such as Gerrit Rietveld and Michel de Klerk.

Floor 1: 1700–1900

Highlights on Floor 1 include the *Battle of Waterloo*, the Rijksmuseum's largest painting (in Gallery 1.12). Three Van Gogh paintings hang in Gallery 1.18. Gallery 1.16 recreates a gilded, 18th-century canal-house room.

Floor 0: 1100–1600

This is an awesome floor for lovers of curiosities and less-visited arts. The Special Collections present peculiar tidbits such as locks, keys, magic lanterns, old dresses, goblets and ship models. The Asia Pavilion, a separate structure that's often devoid of crowds, holds first-rate artworks from China, Indonesia, Japan, India, Thailand and Vietnam.

Facade & Gardens

Pierre Cuypers designed the 1885 building. Check out the exterior, which mixes neo-Gothic and Dutch Renaissance styles. The museum's gardens – aka the 'outdoor gallery' – host big-name sculpture exhibitions at least once per year. They're free to stroll, and offer roses, hedges, fountains and a cool greenhouse year-round.

Top Sights
Vondelpark

New York has Central Park. London has Hyde Park. And Amsterdam has the lush urban idyll of Vondelpark. It's one of Amsterdam's most magical places. On a sunny day, an open-air party atmosphere ensues when tourists, lovers, cyclists, in-line skaters, pram-pushing parents, cartwheeling children, football-kicking teenagers, spliff-sharing friends and champagne-swilling picnickers all come out to play. While the park receives over 10 million visitors per year, it never feels too crowded to enjoy.

Map p96, B3

www.vondelpark.nl

2/5 Hobbemastraat

Statue of Joost van den Vondel, Vondelpark

Don't Miss

Vondel Statue

The English-style gardens, with ponds, lawns, footbridges and winding footpaths, were laid out in 1865 and originally known as Nieuwe Park (New Park). In 1867 sculptor Louis Royer added a **statue** of famed poet and playwright Joost van den Vondel (1587–1679). Amsterdammers began referring to the place as Vondel's Park, which led to it being renamed.

Hippy Remnants

During the late 1960s and early 1970s, Dutch authorities turned the park into a temporary open-air dormitory for the droves of hippies who descended on Amsterdam. The sleeping bags are long gone, but remnants of the era live on in the squats that fringe the park, such as OT301 (p102) and OCCII (p102), now both legalised into underground cultural centres.

Gardens & Grounds

The park's 47 hectares encourage visitors to get out and explore. The **rose garden**, with some 70 different species, was added in 1936. It's in the middle of the park; signs point the way. Neon-green parrots flit through the trees; once pets, they were released into the wild decades ago. The park also shelters several cafes, playgrounds and a wonderful outdoor theatre.

Picasso Sculpture

Art is strewn throughout the park, with 69 sculptures dotted throughout the leafy environs. Among them is Picasso's soaring abstract work *Figure découpée l'Oiseau* (The Bird), better known locally as The Fish (1965), which he donated for the park's centenary.

☑ Top Tips

▶ The main entrance is at the top (north-east) of the park on Stadhouderskade. As you walk southwest, the path splits off to the left or right and makes a complete circle.

▶ The park's flat paths are prime for pedalling. The closest bicycle rental shop is **MacBike** (www.macbike.nl; Weteringschans 2; bike rental per 3/24hr from €7.50/9.25; ☺9am-5.45pm), across the Singel from the main entrance.

▶ Check the schedule at the Openluchttheater (p102), an outdoor stage with free concerts.

✖ Take a Break

Het Groot Melkhuis (p102) is a fairy-tale spot for a drink at the park's edge. For something more architecturally kooky, **'t Blauwe Theehuis** (Map p96, C3; www.blauwetheehuis.nl; Vondelpark 5; ☺9am-10pm; 🛜; 🚋2 Jacob Obreachtstraat) sets up outdoor seats around its flying-saucer-esque building.

Hobbemakade

Hobbemastr

SOUTHERN
CANAL RING

Rijksmuseum
Stadhouderskade
Spiegelgracht

Max
Euweplein

Leidsebosje

Diamond
Museum

Van Gogh
Museum

OUD ZUID

Jan Luijkenstr

House of Bols

Paulus Potterstr

Stedelijk Museum

Jan Willem
Brouwersstr

Honthorststr

Iduanasnplein

Museumplein

Van Baerlestr

Concertgebouwplein

Nicolaas Maesstr

Frans van Mierisstr

Roelof Hartpl

Roelof Hartstr

Gerard Terb

Ruysdaelstr

Banstr

Cornelis Schuytstr

Valeriusstr

Johannes Verhulststr

Noorder Amstel

Reijnier Vinkeles

De Lairessestr

Koninginneweg

Vossiusstr

Vondelstr

Bilderdijkstr

2e Helmersstr

1e Helmersstr

3e Helmersstr

Bosboom Toussaintstr

OUD WEST

2e Constantijn Huygensstr

Jacob van Lennepkanaal

1e Helmersstr

Hollandsche
Manege

Vondelstr

Arie Biemondstr

Jan Pieter Heijestr

Gerard
Brandtstr

Overtoom

Vondelpark

Vondelpark

Koningslaan

Amstelveenseweg

200 m
0.1 miles

For reviews see

◉ Top Sights   p86
◉ Sights   p97
⊗ Eating   p98
⊗ Drinking   p100
☆ Entertainment   p102
⊞ Shopping   p103

Sights

Stedelijk Museum
MUSEUM

1 ⊚ Map p96, D3

Built in 1895 to a neo-Renaissance design by AM Weissman, the Stedelijk Museum is the permanent home of the National Museum of Modern Art. Amassed by postwar curator Willem Sandberg, the modern classics here are among the world's most admired. The permanent collection includes all the blue chips of 19th- and 20th-century painting – Monet, Picasso and Chagall among them – as well as sculptures by Rodin, abstracts by Mondrian and Kandinsky, and much, much more. (⏺573 29 11; www.stedelijk.nl; Museumplein 10; adult/child €15/free, audio guide €5; ⏰10am-6pm Fri-Wed, to 10pm Thu; 🚋2/3/5/12 Van Baerlestraat)

Hollandsche Manege
RIDING SCHOOL

2 ⊚ Map p96, C2

Just outside Vondelpark is the neoclassical Hollandsche Manege, an indoor riding school inspired by the famous Spanish Riding School in Vienna. Designed by AL van Gendt and built in 1882, it retains its charming horse-head facade. Take a riding lesson and/or watch the instructors put the horses through their paces during high tea (€24.50) at the elevated cafe. (⏺618 09 42; www.dehollandschemanege.nl; Vondelstraat 140; adult/child €8/4, private riding lessons per 30min/1hr €37/61; ⏰10am-5pm; 🚋1 1e Constantijn Huygensstraat)

Understand
The Golden Age

The Golden Age spans roughly the 17th century, when Holland was at the peak of its powers. It's the era when Rembrandt painted, when city planners built the canals, and when Dutch ships conquered the seas.

It started when trading rival Antwerp was retaken by the Spaniards in the late 16th century, and merchants, skippers and artisans flocked to Amsterdam. A new moneyed society emerged. Persecuted Jews from Portugal and Spain also fled to Amsterdam. Not only did they introduce the diamond industry, they knew of trade routes to the West and East Indies.

Enter the Dutch East India Company, which wrested the Asian spice trade from the Portuguese. It soon grew into the world's richest corporation, with more than 50,000 employees and a private army. Its sister, the Dutch West India Company, traded with Africa and the Americas and was at the centre of the American slave trade. In 1672 Louis XIV of France invaded the Low Countries, and the brief era known as the Dutch Golden Age ended.

House of Bols

MUSEUM

3 ⊙ Map p96, D2

An hour's self-guided tour through this *jenever* (Dutch gin) museum includes a confusing sniff test, a distilled history of the Bols company, and a cocktail made by one of its formidable bartenders, who train at the academy upstairs. It's kind of cheesy (especially the 'flair booth' where you try out bottle-flipping skills), but fun. On Friday after 5pm admission is €9.50. (www.houseofbols.com; Paulus Potterstraat 14; admission incl 1 cocktail €14.50; ⊙noon-5.30pm Sun-Thu, to 9pm Fri, to 7pm Sat; 🚊2/5 Hobbemastraat)

Local Life
De Hallen Cultural Centre

Locals hobnob at vast, sky-lit **De Hallen** (www.dehallen-amsterdam.nl; Bellamyplein 51; 🚊17 Ten Katestraat), where a cinema, bike recycling store, fashion boutiques and design shops – like Local Goods Store (p103) – pack a century-old tram depot that has undergone a slick revamp. The most popular (and aromatic) facet is the **food hall** (www.foodhallen.nl; Hannie Dankbaar Passage 3, De Hallen; dishes €5-15; ⊙11am-8pm Sun-Wed, to 9pm Thu-Sat; 🚊17 Ten Katestraat). Here more than 20 vendors proffer fare from oysters to chocolate tarts to gourmet croquettes, along with beer and wine. It's a terrific place to hang out for an afternoon, especially if the weather is blustery.

Diamond Museum

MUSEUM

4 ⊙ Map p96, E2

Almost all of the exhibits at the small, low-tech Diamond Museum are clever recreations. Those on a budget can save money by going next door to **Coster Diamonds** (📞305 55 55; www. costerdiamonds.com; Paulus Potterstraat 2; ⊙9am-5pm; 🚊2/5 Hobbemastraat) – the company owns the museum and is attached to it – and taking a free workshop tour, where you can see gem cutters and polishers doing their thing. (www.diamantmuseumamsterdam. nl; Paulus Potterstraat 8; adult/child €8.50/6; ⊙9am-5pm; 🚊2/5 Hobbemastraat)

Eating

Ron Gastrobar

MODERN DUTCH €€

5 🍴 Map p96, A4

Ron Blaauw ran his two-Michelin-star restaurant in these stunning designer premises before trading in the stars to transform the space into an egalitarian 'gastrobar', serving around 25 one-flat-price tapas-style dishes such as steak tartare with crispy veal brains, mushroom ravioli with sweet-potato foam, barbecue-smoked bone marrow, Dutch asparagus with lobster-and-champagne sauce, and Wagyu burgers – with no minimum order restrictions. (📞496 19 43; www. rongastrobar.nl; Sophialaan 55; dishes €15, desserts €9; ⊙noon-2.30pm & 5.30-10.30pm Mon-Fri, noon-10.30pm Sat & Sun; 🛜; 🚊2 Amstelveenseweg)

Dikke Graaf
MEDITERRANEAN €€

6 🍴 Map p96, B2

Heavenly cooking aromas tip you off to this local secret, adorned with copper lamps and black tiling and opening to a terrace. It's a truly fabulous spot for *borrel* (drinks), with gin cocktails, by-the-glass wines and bar snacks such as oysters, bruschetta, charcuterie and manchego sheep's cheese, and/or heartier, nightly changing meat, fish and pasta dishes. (📞223 77 56; www.dikkegraaf.nl; Wilhelminastraat 153; bar snacks €3.50-15, mains €12.50-22.50; 🕑kitchen 3-10pm Wed-Sun; 🚊1 Rhijnvis Feithstraat)

Adam
GASTRONOMY €€

7 🍴 Map p96, A3

Widely tipped around town for a Michelin star, this chic restaurant serves exquisitely presented gastronomic fare, such as steak tartare with quail's egg, crispy pork belly with celeriac, sea bass with white asparagus, and *côte de bœuf* (on-the-bone rib steak) for two. Dessert is either a cheese platter or a chef's surprise. Paired wines are available for €7.50 per glass. (📞233 98 52; www.restaurantadam.nl; Overtoom 515; mains €21-24.50, 3-/4-/5-/6-course menus €35/42.50/50/57.50; 🕑6-10.30pm Tue-Sat; 🚊1 Overtoomsesluis)

Braai BBQ Bar
BARBECUE €

8 🍴 Map p96, A3

A canal-side *haringhuis* (herring stand) has been brilliantly converted into a street-food-style barbecue bar.

Snacks span sandwiches such as hummus and grilled veggies or smoked *ossenworst* (raw-beef sausage originating from Amsterdam), a cheese and bacon burger and Braai's speciality – marinated, barbecued ribs (half or full rack). PIN cards are preferred, but it accepts cash. Tables scatter under the trees. (www.braaiamsterdam.nl; Schinkelhavenkade 1; dishes €5-11; 🕑11am-10pm; 🚊1 Overtoomsesluis)

Narbonne
BISTRO €€

9 🍴 Map p96, D1

A neighbourhood treasure, down-to-earth Narbonne serves main courses such as lamb shank with baked garlic potatoes, but the reason it's locally loved is its tapas, such as smoked mozzarella tortellini, fried manchego sheep's cheese, marinated artichokes, prawns in filo pastry, fresh oysters with lime and chive dressing, green-olive tapenade with crusty bread, and grilled beef skewers. Book ahead. (📞618 32 63; www.narbonne.nl; Bosboom Toussaintstraat 28; tapas €4.50-14, mains €16-23; 🕑5.30-11pm Tue-Sun; 🚊1 1e Constantijn Huygensstraat)

l'Entrecôte et les Dames
FRENCH €€

10 🍴 Map p96, D3

With a double-height wall made from wooden drawers and a wrought-iron-balustraded mezzanine seating area, the decor is stunning – but still secondary to the food. The two-course dinner menu offers a meat or fish option, but everyone's here for the entrecôte (premium beef steak). Save room for scrumptious desserts: perhaps chocolate mousse, *tarte au citron* (lemon tart) or *crêpes au Grand Marnier*. (☑679 88 88; www.entrecote-et-les-dames. nl; Van Baerlestraat 47-49; lunch mains €12.50, 2-course dinner menu €24; ☉noon-3pm & 5.30-10pm; ☐16/24 Museumplein)

La Falote
DUTCH €€

11 Map p96, E4

Wee La Falote, with its chequered tablecloths, focuses on daily changing Dutch home-style dishes such as calf liver, meatballs with endives, or stewed fish with beets and mustard sauce. The prices are a bargain in an otherwise ritzy neighbourhood; and wait till the owner brings out the accordion. Cash only. (☑662 54 54; www.lafalote.nl; Roelof Hartstraat 26; mains €15-23; ☉2-9pm Mon-Sat; ☐3/5/12/24 Roelof Hartplein)

Restaurant Blauw
INDONESIAN €€€

12 Map p96, A4

The *New York Times* voted Blauw the 'best Indonesian restaurant in the Netherlands' and legions agree, because the large, contemporary dining room is always packed (reserve well ahead). Menu standouts include *ikan pesmol* (fried fish with candlenut sauce) and *ayam singgand* (chicken in semi-spicy coconut sauce with tumeric leaf) and mouthwatering Indonesian desserts. (☑675 50 00; www.restaurant blauw.nl; Amstelveenseweg 158; mains €21.50-27.50, rijsttafel per person €26.50-31.50; ☉6-10.30pm Mon-Fri, 5-10.30pm Sat & Sun; ☐2 Amstelveenseweg)

Drinking

Franklin
COCKTAIL BAR

13 Map p96, A4

Creative cocktails at this split-level, stained-glass-windowed bar include Picnic at Vondel (lemon-infused gin, summer fruit syrup and chardonnay), Smoke on the Water (*mezcal*, lime syrup and dandelion bitters) and a Porn Star Martini (vanilla-infused vodka, passion-fruit purée and *prosecco*). Warm evenings see its summer terrace get packed to capacity – arrive early to get a seat. (www.barfranklin.nl; Amstelveenseweg 156; ☉5pm-1am Tue-Thu, to 3am Fri & Sat; ☐2 Amstelveenseweg)

Craft & Draft
BEER CAFÉ

14 Map p96, B3

Craft beer fans are spoilt for choice, with no fewer than 40 different beers on tap. A huge blackboard chalks up each day's draught – or draft – offerings, such as Belgian 3 Floyds' Lips of Faith, American Coronado's Stupid Stout and Evil Twin's Yang, British Red Willow's Thoughtless, Swedish Sigtuna's Organic Ale and Danish Mikkeller's Peter, Pale & Mary. (www.craftanddraft.nl; Overtoom 417; ☉bar 2pm-midnight Sun-Thu, to 2am Fri & Sat, shop 2-10pm daily; ☐1 Rhijnvis Feithstraat)

Lot Sixty One
COFFEE

15 Map p96, C1

Look downstairs to the open cellar to see (and better yet, smell) coffee being roasted at this streetwise spot. Beans

House of Bols (p98)

are sourced from individual ecofriendly farms; varieties include Ethiopian Tchembe, Tanzanian Aranga, Colombian Gerado, Costa Rican Don Mayo, Guatemalan Maravilla and Rwandan Mahembe. All coffees are double shots (unless you specify otherwise); watch Kinkerstraat's passing parade from benches out front. (www.lotsixtyonecoffee. com; Kinkerstraat 112; ⏱8am-5pm Mon-Fri, 9am-5pm Sat, 10am-5pm Sun; 🚊3/12 Bilderdijkstraat)

Café Bédier

BROWN CAFÉ

16 🚇 Map p96, A4

At the end of the work day, the terrace out the front of Café Bédier is often so crowded it looks like a street party

in full swing. Inside, the leather-upholstered wall panels, modular seats and hardwood floors put a 21st-century twist on classic brown-*café* decor. Top-notch bar food, too. (📞662 44 15; Sophialaan 36; ⏱noon-1am Mon-Thu, to 3am Fri, 11am-3am Sat, to 1am Sun; 🚊2 Amstelveenseweg)

BarBrå

BAR

17 🚇 Map p96, B2

Not, perhaps, what the name might suggest (*brå* means 'good' in Swedish and Norwegian), this cosy hang-out with mismatched, recycled furniture and industrial light fittings feels more like a party in someone's apartment, with comfy vintage sofas, armchairs, and stools around the bar. There's a mini terrace out front, but it's so popular it's usually standing room only out there. (www.bar-bra.nl; Jan Pieter Heijestraat 137; ⏰4pm-midnight Wed & Thu, 10am-3am Fri & Sat, to 11pm Sun; 🚊1 Jan Pieter Heijestraat)

Het Groot Melkhuis
CAFE

18 🚇 Map p96, C3

At the edge of the Vondelpark's forest, this huge Swiss-chalet-style timber house appears like something out of a fairytale. The vast drinking and dining forecourt and playground cater to families (and all kid-like guests). (📞612 96 74; www.grootmelkhuis.nl; Vondelpark 2; ⏰10am-6pm; 📶👶; 🚊1 Jan Pieter Heijestraat)

Entertainment

Concertgebouw
CLASSICAL MUSIC

19 ⭐ Map p96, D3

Bernard Haitink, former conductor of the venerable Royal Concertgebouw Orchestra, once remarked that the world-famous hall – built in 1888 with near-perfect acoustics – was the orchestra's best instrument. Free half-hour concerts take place every Wednesday at 12.30pm from mid-September to late June; arrive early. Try the Last Minute Ticket Shop (p80) for half-price seats to all other performances. (📞671 83 45; www.concertgebouw.nl; Concertgebouwplein 10;

⏰box office 1-7pm Mon-Fri, 10am-7pm Sat & Sun; 🚊3/5/12/16/24 Museumplein)

Openluchttheater
THEATRE

20 ⭐ Map p96, C3

Each summer the Vondelpark hosts free concerts in its intimate open-air theatre. It's a fantastic experience to share with others. Expect world music, dance, theatre and more. You can make a reservation (€5 per seat) on the website up to two hours in advance of showtime. (Open-Air Theatre; www.openluchttheater.nl; Vondelpark 5a; ⏰May–mid-Sep; 👶; 🚊1 1e Constantijn Huygensstraat)

OT301
LIVE MUSIC

21 ⭐ Map p96, B2

Graffiti-covered ex-squat OT301, in the former Netherlands Film Academy, hosts an eclectic roster of bands and DJs. There are two bars as well as vegan restaurant De Peper (📞412 29 54; www.depeper.org; mains €7-10; 7-8.30pm Tue, Thu, Fri & Sun), serving cheap, organic, vegan meals in a lovable dive-bar atmosphere. Sit at the communal table to connect with like-minded folk. Same-day reservations are required; call between 3pm and 6.30pm. (www.ot301.nl; Overtoom 301; 🚊1 Jan Pieter Heijestraat)

OCCII
LIVE MUSIC

22 ⭐ Map p96, A4

Former squat OCCII maintains a thriving alternative scene, and books underground bands, many from Amsterdam. Vegan fare is served at its

Eetcafé MKZ (📞 679 07 12; www.binnenpr. home.xs4all.nl/mkz.htm; 1e Schinkelstraat 16; mains from €5; 🕐from 7pm Tue-Fri; 🍴; 🚊2 Amstelveenseweg), a collectively run, no-frills restaurant. Call between 2.30pm and 6pm to reserve your spot and confirm prices for the changing vegan meals, but be sure to arrive early, as once the food's gone, that's it. (📞 671 77 78; www.occii.org; Amstelveenseweg 134; 🕐hours vary; ♿; 🚊2 Amstelveenseweg)

Shopping

Local Goods Store   HANDICRAFTS

23 🔒 Map p96, B1

As the name implies, everything at this concept shop inside De Hallen is created by Dutch designers. Look for Woody skateboards, I Made Gin gin production kits, Carhusa purses and handbags, Timbies wooden bow ties, Lucila Kenny hand-dyed scarves and jewellery, and Neef Louis industrial vintage homewares, as well as racks of great Dutch-designed casual men's and women's fashion. (www.localgoods store.nl; Hannie Dankbaar Passage 39, De Hallen; 🕐noon-7pm Tue-Fri & Sun, 11am-7pm Sat; 🚊17 Ten Katestraat)

Pied à Terre   BOOKS

24 🔒 Map p96, C2

The galleried, sky-lit interior of Europe's largest travel bookshop feels like a Renaissance centre of learning. If it's travel or outdoor-related, it's likely here: gorgeous globes, travel guides in

☑️ Top Tip

Museum Shop at the Museumplein

The Van Gogh Museum and Rijksmuseum jointly operate the **Museum Shop at the Museumplein** (Hobbemastraat; 🕐shop 10am-6pm, ticket window for museum entrance 8.30am-6pm; 🚊2/5 Hobbemastraat), so you can pick up posters, notecards and other art souvenirs from both institutions in one fell swoop (and avoid the museums' entrance queues).

multiple languages (especially English) and over 600,000 maps. Order a coffee and dream up your next trip at the cafe tables. (📞 627 44 55; www.piedaterre. nl; Overtoom 135-137; 🕐1-6pm Mon, 10am-6pm Tue, Wed & Fri, to 9pm Thu, to 5pm Sat; 🚊1 1e Constantijn Huygensstraat)

Edha Interieur   HOMEWARES

25 🔒 Map p96, D3

You might not end up buying a sofa, kitchen unit or bathroom suite in these three neighbouring 19th-century buildings, but Edha is one of the best places in town to check out cutting-edge Dutch design. Smaller items more suitable to pack in your luggage (or at least ship) include textiles, groovy lights and kitchen gadgets. (www.edha-interieur.nl; Willemsparkweg 5-9; 🕐10am-6pm Tue-Sat; 🚊2/3/5/12 Van Baerlestraat)

Explore

De Pijp

With its narrow streets crowded by a lively mix of people – labourers, intellectuals, new immigrants, prostitutes, young urban professionals, gays, movie stars – De Pijp is Amsterdam's most spontaneous and creative quarter. Aside from the Heineken brewery tour, there aren't many sights. But free-spirited *cafés* and groovy restaurants on every block? That's where De Pijp rocks it.

The Sights in a Day

☀ Brunch is a big to-do in De Pijp, so start off with a bountiful morning feed at **Bakers & Roasters** (p110) or **Scandinavian Embassy** (p111). Then browse the cool shops. **Hutspot** (p115) features Dutch design decor. Fashion buffs can browse the vintage wares at **Kolifleur** (p115).

☼ For lunch grab a burger at **Butcher** (p111). Not hungry after the big breakfast? Opt for a coffee pick-me-up at **Café de Groene Vlinder** (p114). Then prepare for the **Heineken Experience** (p109), the multimedia brewery tour where you'll get shaken up, bottled and 'become' a beer. If you go in the late afternoon, the tasting at the end provides a built-in happy hour.

☾ You're spoiled for choice come dinnertime. There's **Volt** (p110) for Mediterranean bites under twinkling lights or **Restaurant Elmar** (p111) for locavore Dutch dishes in the courtyard garden. In the evening, catch a show at **CC Muziekcafé** (p114) or settle in for housemade beer at **Brouwerij Troost** (p112) or organic wine at **Glouglou** (p112).

For a local's day in De Pijp, see p106.

🔍 Local Life
Discovering Bohemian De Pijp (p106)

❤ Best of Amsterdam
Shopping
Albert Cuypmarkt (p106; pictured opposite)

Eating
Restaurant Elmar (p111)
Dèsa (p112)
Fat Dog (p110)
Butcher (p111)
Bakers & Roasters (p110)
Scandinavian Embassy (p111)

Drinking & Nightlife
Brouwerij Troost (p112)
Glouglou (p112)

Getting There

🚋 **Tram** Trams 16 and 24 roll along Ferdinand Bolstraat by De Pijp's main sights, all the way from Centraal Station.

Ⓜ **Metro** When it opens in 2017, the Noord/Zuidlijn (north–south) metro line will have a De Pijp station with entrances on the corner of Ferdinand Bolstraat and Albert Cuypstraat, and Ferdinand Bolstraat and Ceintuurbaan.

Local Life
Discovering Bohemian De Pijp

Artists and intellectuals have hung out in De Pijp since the 19th century, when the former slum's cheap housing drew them in. The district still wafts bohemian flair, from the spicy market at its epicentre to the cool-cat cafes and retro shops that jam its streets. A surprise red-light area also makes an appearance.

❶ Albert Cuypmarkt

This is Amsterdam's largest and busiest **market** (www.albertcuypmarkt.nl; Albert Cuypstraat, btwn Ferdinand Bolstraat & Van Woustraat; ⊙9am-5pm Mon-Sat; 🚊16/24 Albert Cuypstraat) Vendors from Indonesia, Suriname, Morocco and other countries loudly tout their gadgets, clothing and spices, while Dutch snack stalls tempt with herring sandwiches and caramel-syrup-filled

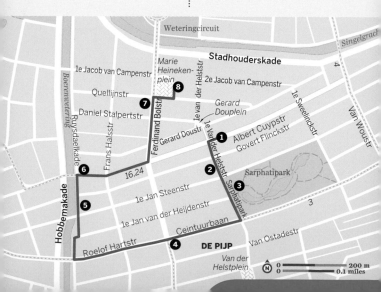

stroopwafels. Graze as you gaze at the whirl of goods on offer.

❷ Katsu

Relaxed **Katsu** (www.katsu.nl; 1e Van der Helststraat 70; ⏰10am-midnight Mon-Thu, 10am-1am Fri & Sat, 11am-midnight Sun; 🚊16/24 Albert Cuypstraat), De Pijp's favourite coffeeshop, brims with colourful characters of all ages and dispositions. The front table with newspapers lends a bookish vibe. When seating on the ground floor and terrace gets tight, head up to the 1st-floor lounge.

❸ Sarphatipark

While the Vondelpark is bigger in size and reputation, **Sarphatipark** (Ceintuurbaan; 🚊16/24 Albert Cuypstraat) delivers an equally potent shot of pastoral relaxation, with far fewer crowds. In the centre is a bombastic temple with a fountain, gargoyles and a bust of Samuel Sarphati (1813–66), a Jewish doctor, businessman and urban innovator who helped define the neighbourhood.

❹ CT Coffee & Coconuts

CT Coffee & Coconuts (www.ctamsterdam.nl; Ceintuurbaan 282-284; mains €6.50-21.50; ⏰7am-11pm Mon-Fri, from 8am Sat & Sun; 🛜; 🚊3 Ceintuurbaan) spreads through a cathedral-like building that was once a 1920s art-deco cinema. Locals flock here for fab brunch dishes such as coconut, almond and buckwheat pancakes and French-toast brioche with apricots. The lunch and dinner menu spans prawn tacos and tempeh burgers.

❺ Red-Light Area

What the...? You're walking along Ruysdaelkade and suddenly there's a strip of **red-light windows** between 1e Jan Steenstraat and Albert Cuypstraat. It's a good place to glimpse the world's oldest profession, minus the stag parties and drunken crowds that prowl the main Red Light District.

❻ Café Binnen Buiten

The minute there's a sliver of sunshine, **Café Binnen Buiten** (www.cafebinnen buiten.nl; Ruysdaelkade 115; ⏰11am-1am Sun-Thu, to 3am Fri & Sat; 🚊16/24 Ruysdaelkade) gets packed. Sure, the food's good and the bar is candlelit and cosy. But what really brings the crowds is simply the best canal-side terrace in De Pijp.

❼ Record Mania

Fantastically old-school, **Record Mania** (www.recordmania.nl; Ferdinand Bolstraat 30; ⏰noon-6pm Mon-Sat; 🚊16/24 Stadhouderskade) is where neighbourhood folks go for their vinyl and CDs. The shop, with old posters, stained-glass windows, and records and CDs embedded in the floor, is a treasure in itself.

❽ Barça

One of the hottest bars in De Pijp, **Barça** (www.barca.nl; Marie Heinekenplein 30-31; ⏰11am-1am Sun-Thu, to 3am Fri & Sat; 🚊16/24 Stadhouderskade) – themed 'Barcelona in Amsterdam' – is the heartbeat of Marie Heinekenplein. Hang out in the plush-gold and dark-timber interior, or spread out onto the terrace, glass of sparkling wine in hand.

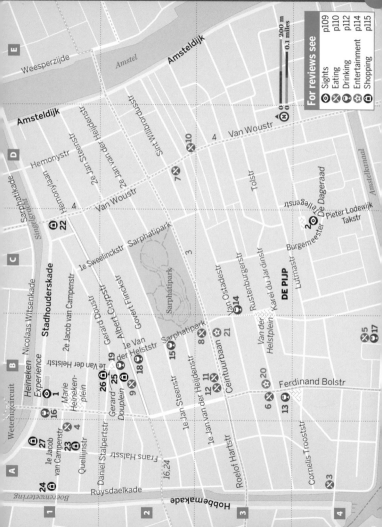

Weesperzijde

Amstel

Amsteldijk

Amsteldijk

Van Woustr

Hemonystr

Hemonylaan

2e Jan Steenstr

Sint Willibrordusstr

2e Jan van der Heijdenstr

Van Woustr

Tolstr

De Dageraad

Pieter Lodewijk Takstr

Burgemeester

De Pieter Bellengastr

Sarphatikade

Singelgracht

Stadhouderskade

Nicolaas Witsenkade

1e Sweelinckstr

Sarphatipark

Sarphatipark

3

Karel du Jardinstr

Van Ostadestr

Rustenburgerstr

Lutmastr

DE PIJP

Amstelkanaal

Heineken Experience

2e Jacob van Campenstr

Gerard Doustr

Albert Cuypstr

Govert Flinckstr

1e Van der Helststr

Sarphatipark

Van der Helstplein

Marie Heinekenplein

1e Jan Steenstr

1e Jan van der Heijdenstr

Ceintuurbaan

Ferdinand Bolstr

Weteringcircuit

1e Jacob van Campenstr

Quellijnstr

Daniël Stalpertstr

Frans Halsstr

Ruysdaelkade

Gerard Douplein

Roelof Hartstr

Cornelis Trooststr

Hobbemakade

Boerenwetering

200 m
0.1 miles

Sights

Heineken Experience BREWERY

1 Map p108, B1

On the site of the company's old brewery, the crowning glory of this self-guided 'Experience' (samples aside) is a multimedia exhibit where you 'become' a beer by getting shaken up, sprayed with water and subjected to heat. True beer connoisseurs will shudder, but it's a lot of fun. Admission includes a 15-minute shuttle-boat ride to the **Heineken Brand Store** (www.heinekenthecity.nl; Amstelstraat 31; ☺noon-6pm Mon, from 10am Tue-Sun; 🚊4/9/14 Rembrandtplein) near Rembrandtplein. Prebooking tickets online saves you €2 on the entry fee and allows you to skip the ticket queues. (📞523 92 22; www.heinekenexperience.com; Stadhouderskade 78; adult/child €18/12.50; ☺10.30am-9pm Jul & Aug, to 7.30pm Mon-Thu, to 9pm Fri-Sun Sep-Jun; 🚊16/24 Stadhouderskade)

De Dageraad ARCHITECTURE

2 Map p108, C4

Following the key Housing Act of 1901, which forced the city to rethink neighbourhood planning and condemn slums, De Dageraad housing estate was developed between 1918 and 1923 for poorer families. One of the most original architects of the expressionist Amsterdam School, Piet Kramer, drew up plans for this idiosyncratic complex in collaboration with Michel de Klerk (Dawn Housing Project; Pieter Lodewijk Takstraat; 🚊4 Amstelkade)

Understand
Amsterdam School Architecture

When Amsterdam School architecture started around WWI, it was as much a political movement as an aesthetic one. Architects such as Pieter Kramer and Michel de Klerk were reacting to the lavish, decadent style of neo-Renaissance buildings like Centraal Station, but also to appalling housing conditions for the poor. Their fantastical public-funded housing projects resemble shells, waves and other organic forms; they were obsessive about details, designing everything down to the house numbers. Some details were a bit paternalistic and controlling – windows high in the wall were meant to deter leaning out and gossiping with neighbours – but in general the buildings were vast improvements. The best examples to see are De Dageraad in De Pijp and Museum Het Schip (p65) near Westerpark.

Eating

Fat Dog
HOT DOGS €

3 🍴 Map p108, A4

Uberchef Ron Blaauw, of Ron Gastrobar (p98), elevates the humble hot dog to an art form. Ultra-gourmet options include Naughty Bangkok (pickled vegetables, red curry mayo, and dry crispy rice); Vive La France (fried mushrooms, foie gras and truffle mayo); Gangs of New York (sauerkraut, bacon, and smoked-onion marmalade) and Vega Gonzalez (vegetarian sausage, corn, guacamole, sour cream and jalapeño mayo). (www.thefatdog.nl; Ruysdaelkade 251; dishes €4.50-12; ⏲5pm-midnight Mon & Tue, from noon Wed-Sun; 🚊12 Cornelis Troostplein)

Bakers & Roasters
CAFE €

4 🍴 Map p108, A1

Sumptuous brunch dishes served up at Brazilian/Kiwi-owned Bakers & Roasters include banana nutbread French toast with homemade banana marmalade and crispy bacon; Navajo eggs with pulled pork, avocado, mango salsa and chipotle cream; and a smoked salmon stack with poached eggs, potato cakes and hollandaise. Wash them down with a fiery Bloody Mary. Fantastic pies, cakes and slices, too. (bakersandroasters.com; 1e Jacob van Campenstraat 54; dishes €7.50-15.50; ⏲8.30am-4pm; 🚊16/24 Stadhouderskade)

Ciel Bleu
FRENCH €€€

5 🍴 Map p108, B4

Mindblowing, two-Michelin-star creations at this pinnacle of gastronomy change with the seasons, so springtime might see scallops and oysters with vanilla sea salt and gin-and-tonic foam, king crab with salted lemon, beurre blanc ice cream and caviar, or saddle of lamb with star anise. Just as incomparable is the 23rd-floor setting with aerial views north across the city. (📞450 67 87; www.okura.nl; Ferdinand Bolstraat 333, Hotel Okura Amsterdam; mains €60, 7-course menu €110, with paired wines €170; ⏲6.30-10.30pm Mon-Sat, closed late Jul–mid-Aug; 🚊12 Cornelius Trootsplein)

Volt
MEDITERRANEAN €€

6 🍴 Map p108, B3

Strung with coloured lightbulbs, Volt is a neighbourhood gem for light tapas-style bites (olives and marinated sardines; aioli and tapenade) and more substantial mains (artichoke ravioli with walnuts and ruccola; squid stuffed with chorizo and rice; and plaice with mozzarella risotto croquette. Its bar stays open until late, or head across the street to **Gambrinus** (www.gambrinus.nl; Ferdinand Bolstraat 180; ⏲11am-1am Sun-Thu, to 3am Fri & Sat; 📶; 🚊12 Cornelis Troostplein), its brown-*café* sibling. (📞471 55 44; www.restaurantvolt.nl; Ferdinand Bolstraat 178; mains €14-20, tapas €4-14; ⏲4-10pm; 🚊12 Cornelis Troostplein)

Restaurant Elmar
MODERN DUTCH €€

7 🍴 Map p108, D2

Seriously good cooking at this charming little locavore restaurant utilises organic Dutch produce (Flevopolder beef, Texel lamb, Noord-Holland pigs, polder chickens and locally milled flour, along with seasonal fruit and vegetables). Original flavour combinations include ham-wrapped chicken stuffed with liver and sage in marsala jus, and bitter-chocolate mousse with apple compote and iced-coffee foam. There's a delightful courtyard garden. (📞664 66 29; www.restaurantelmar.nl; Van Woustraat 110; mains lunch €7.50-12.50, dinner €19.50-24.50; 🕑noon-3pm & 6-10pm Tue-Sat; 🚊4 Ceintuurbaan)

Scandinavian Embassy
CAFE €

8 🍴 Map p108, B3

Oatmeal porridge with blueberries, honey and coconut, served with goat's milk yoghurt; salt-cured salmon on Danish rye with sheep's milk yoghurt; muesli with strawberries; and freshly baked pastries, including cinnamon buns, make this blond-wood-panelled spot a perfect place to start the day. As does its phenomenal coffee sourced from Scandinavian micro-roasteries (including a refreshing cold-brewed coffee with tonic water). (scandinavianembassy.nl; Sarphatipark 34; dishes €4.40-12; 🕑8am-6pm Mon-Fri, 10am-5pm Sat & Sun; 🚊3 2e Van der Helststraat)

Local Life
Picnic in the Park

Great places to pick up supplies for a picnic in Sarphatipark include **'t Kaasboertje** (Gerard Doustraat 60; 1-5.30pm Mon, 🕑9am-5.30pm Tue-Fri, 9am-4pm Sat; 🚊16/24 Stadhouderskade), a cheese shop where wheels of Gouda line the walls along with crispbreads, crackers and regional wines, and **Beer Tree** (www.thebeertree.nl; 1e Van der Helststraat 53; 🕑noon-10pm; 🚊16/24 Albert Cuypstraat), which sells more than 250 different craft beers from around the globe.

Butcher
BURGERS €

9 🍴 Map p108, B2

Burgers at this sizzling spot are cooked right in front of you (behind a glass screen, so you won't get splattered). Mouthwatering choices include 'Silence of the Lamb' (with spices and tahini), the 'Codfather' (beer-battered blue cod and homemade tartare sauce), an Angus beef truffle burger and a veggie version. Ask about its secret cocktail bar. (📞470 78 75; www.the-butcher.com; Albert Cuypstraat 129; burgers €6.50-12.50; 🕑11am-late; 🚻; 🚊16/24 Albert Cuypstraat)

Spaghetteria
ITALIAN €€

10 🍴 Map p108, D2

Freshly made pastas at this hip, Italian-run 'pasta bar' come in six daily options that might include ricotta and walnut ravioli; spaghetti with calamari in spicy tomato sauce; squid-ink linguine with pesto and spinach; and ham tortellini in creamy goat's-cheese sauce. The huge wooden communal table (and wine) adds to the electric atmosphere. There's another branch near Vondelpark. (www. spaghetteria-pastabar.nl; Van Woustraat 123; pasta €9-14; ☉5-10.15pm; 📮4 Ceintuurbaan)

Friterie par Hasard
DUTCH €€

11 ✖ Map p108, B3

Fronted by a red-and-white chequered awning, low-lit Friterie par Hasard is feted for its *frites* (fries), served with dishes like ribs in traditional Limburg stew with apple, elderberry and bay leaf sauce; marinated chicken thighs with satay sauce and pickled cucumber; bavette steak; and beer-battered cod. Its adjacent **Frites uit Zuyd** (www.fritesuit zuyd.nl; Ceintuurbaan; dishes €3-5.50; ☉noon-10pm Sun & Mon, to 11pm Tue-Thu, to midnight Fri & Sat; 📮3 Ferdinand Bolstraat) fries up takeaway *frites*. (www.cafeparhasard.nl; Ceintuurbaan 113; mains €17.50, 3-course menu €27.50; ☉noon-10pm Sun-Thu, to 10.30pm Fri & Sat; 📮3 Ferdinand Bolstraat)

Dèsa
INDONESIAN €€

12 ✖ Map p108, B3

Named for the Indonesian word for 'village' (apt for this city, but especially this 'hood), Dèsa is wildly popular for its *rijsttafel* ('rice table') banquets. À la carte options include *serundeng* (spiced fried coconut), *ayam besengek* (chicken cooked in saffron and coconut milk), *sambal goreng telor* (stewed eggs in spicy Balinese sauce), and *pisang*

goreng (fried banana) for dessert. (☏671 09 79; www.restaurantdesa.com; Ceintuurbaan 103; mains €12.50-14.50, rijst-tafel €15.20-32; ☉5-10.30pm; 📮3 Ferdinand Bolstraat)

Drinking

Brouwerij Troost
BREWERY

13 🍺 Map p108, B3

Watch beer being brewed in copper vats at this outstanding craft brewery. Its dozen beers include a summery blonde, smoked porter, strong tripel, and deep-red Imperial IPA; it also distils gin from its beer and serves fantastic bar food including humongous burgers. Troost's popularity (book ahead on weekend evenings) saw its second **premises** (☏737 10 28; www.brouwerijtroostwestergas. nl; Pazzanistraat 27, Westergasfabriek; ☉4pm-1am Mon-Thu, 4pm-3am Fri, noon-3am Sat, noon-midnight Sun; 📶; 📮10 Van Limburg Stirumstraat) open in Westergasfabriek. (☏737 10 28; www.brouwerijtroost.nl; Cornelis Troostplein 21; ☉4pm-1am Mon-Thu, 4pm-3am Fri, 2pm-3am Sat, 2pm-midnight Sun; 📶; 📮12 Cornelis Troostplein)

Glouglou
WINE BAR

14 🍺 Map p108, C3

Natural, all-organic, additive-free wines are the stock-in-trade of this convivial neighbourhood wine bar in a rustic stained-glass-framed shop, where the party often spills out into the street. More than 40 well-priced French wines are available by the glass; it also sells bottles to drink on-site or take away.

Sarphatipark (p107)

(www.glouglou.nl; 2e Van der Helststraat 3;
⏱4pm-midnight Mon-Fri, from 3pm Sat & Sun;
🚊3 2e Van der Helststraat)

Boca's
BAR

15 🚊 Map p108, B2

Boca's (Italian for 'mouth') is the
ultimate spot for *borrel* (drinks).
Mezzanine seating overlooks the
cushion-strewn interior but in
summer the best seats are on the
terrace facing leafy Sarphatipark. Its
pared-down wine list (seven by-the-
glass choices) goes perfectly with its
lavish sharing platters. (www.bar-bocas.
nl; Sarphatipark 4; ⏱10am-1am Mon-Thu,
10am-3am Fri & Sat, 11am-1am Sun; 🛜; 🚊3
2e Van der Helststraat)

Café Berkhout
BROWN CAFÉ

16 🚊 Map p108, B1

With its dark wood, mirrored and
chandelier-rich splendour and shabby
elegance, this brown *café* is a natural
post–Heineken Experience wind-down
spot (it's right across the street). Great
food too, especially burgers. (www.cafe
berkhout.nl; Stadhouderskade 77; ⏱10am-
1am Mon-Thu, to 3am Fri & Sat, 11am-1am Sun;
🛜; 🚊16/24 Stadhouderskade)

Twenty Third Bar
COCKTAIL BAR

17 🚊 Map p108, B4

Twenty Third Bar has sweeping views
to the west and south, a stunning bar-
snack menu prepared in the kitchen

Local Life
Café Sarphaat
Grab an outdoor table along Sarphatipark, order a frothy beer and see if you don't feel like a local. **Café Sarphaat** (☑675 15 65; Ceintuurbaan 157; ⏰9am-1am Sun-Thu, to 3am Fri & Sat; ☑3/4 Van Woustraat) is one of the neighbourhood's best spots, with a lovely old bar that makes sipping a *jenever* (Dutch gin) seem natural.

---

of Ciel Bleu (p110; dishes €9 to €18; caviar €36 to €60 per 10g), champagne cocktails and Heineken on tap. (www.okura.nl; Ferdinand Bolstraat 333, Hotel Okura Amsterdam; ⏰6pm-1am Sun-Thu, to 2am Fri & Sat; ☑12 Cornelius Trootsplein)

Café de Groene Vlinder
BROWN CAFÉ

Right on Albert Cuypstraat near Chocolate Bar (see **18** ☻ Map p108, B2), the Green Butterfly strikes just the right balance between hip and *gezellig* (cosy, convivial), making it perfect for a *koffie verkeerd* (milky coffee) in the warm wood interior or a *biertje* (beer) on the buzzing patio. (www.cafe-de-groene-vlinder.nl; Albert Cuypstraat 130; ⏰10am-1am Sun-Thu, to 3am Fri & Sat; ☑16/24 Albert Cuypstraat)

Chocolate Bar
DESIGNER BAR

18 ☻ Map p108, B2

Chocolate isn't the draw here – it's the cool vibe, retro '60s/'70s interior and

Euro soundtrack. The candlelit bar makes it feel like a night out even at noon. On chilly days, curl up with a woolly blanket on the patio. At night, DJs hit the decks from Thursday to Sunday. (www.chocolate-bar.nl; 1e Van der Helststraat 62a; ⏰9am-1am Sun-Thu, to 3am Fri & Sat; ☑16/24 Albert Cuypstraat)

Pilsvogel
BROWN CAFÉ

19 ☻ Map p108, B2

The kitchen dispenses small plates through to full meals but that's really secondary when you're sitting on De Pijp's most festive corner, on one of the neighbourhood's prime people-watching patios. (www.pilsvogel.nl; Gerard Douplein 14; ⏰10am-1am Sun-Thu, to 3am Fri & Sat; ☑16/24 Albert Cuypstraat)

Entertainment

CC Muziekcafé
LIVE MUSIC

20 ☆ Map p108, B3

A feel-good little club right at home in De Pijp. It dishes up weekly and monthly themed music nights from reggae to soul to rock. (www.cccafe.nl; Rustenburgerstraat 384; ⏰8pm-1am Sun-Thu, to 3am Fri & Sat; 🛜; ☑12 Cornelis Troostplein)

Rialto Cinema
CINEMA

21 ☆ Map p108, B3

This great old cinema near Sarphatipark focuses on premieres, and shows eclectic, art-house fare from around the world (foreign films feature Dutch subtitles). There are three screens and a stylish cafe. (📞676 87 00; www.rialtofilm.nl; Ceintuurbaan 338; adult/child from €9/7.50; 🚊3 2e Van der Helststraat)

Shopping

Hutspot
CONCEPT STORE

22 🔒 Map p108, C1

Named after the Dutch dish of boiled and mashed vegies, 'Hotchpotch' was founded by four young guys with a mission to give young entrepreneurs the chance to sell their work. As a result, this concept store is an inspired mishmash of Dutch-designed furniture, furnishings, art, homewares and clothing plus a cool in-store cafe and bar. (www.hutspotamsterdam.com; Van Woustraat 4; ⏰shop & cafe 10am-7pm Mon-Sat, noon-6pm Sun, bar 5pm-1am Mon-Thu, 4pm-3am Fri & Sat, 4pm-1am Sun; 🚊4 Stadhouderskade)

Kolifleur
VINTAGE

23 🔒 Map p108, A1

Mint-condition, secondhand designer clothing, jewellery and bags by Dutch designers are the stock-in-trade of funky Kolifleur, along with vintage furniture and homewares. (kolifleur.nl; Frans Halsstraat 35; ⏰11am-7pm Tue-Sat; 🚊16/24 Albert Cuypstraat)

Tiller Galerie
ART

24 🔒 Map p108, A1

This intimate, friendly gallery has works by George Heidweiller (check

out the surreal Amsterdam skyscapes), Peter Donkersloot's portraits of animals and iconic actors like Marlon Brando, and Herman Brood prints. (www.tillergalerie.com; 1e Jacob van Campenstraat 1; ⏰1-7pm Thu & Fri, to 5pm Sat & Sun, by appointment Wed; 🚊16/24 Stadhouderskade)

Brick Lane
FASHION

25 🔒 Map p108, B2

Individual, affordable designs arrive at this London-inspired boutique every couple of weeks, keeping the selection up-to-the-minute. (www.bricklane-amsterdam.nl; Gerard Doustraat 783; ⏰1-6pm Mon, 10.30am-6pm Tue-Sat, 12.30-5.30pm Sun; 🚊16/24 Albert Cuypstraat)

Raak
CLOTHING

26 🔒 Map p108, B2

Unique casual clothing, bags, jewellery and homewares by Dutch and Scandinavian designers fill Raak's shelves and racks. (www.raakamsterdam.nl; 1e Van der Helststraat 46; ⏰noon-6pm Mon, from 10am Tue-Sat; 🚊16/24 Albert Cuypstraat)

Van Beek
ARTS

27 🔒 Map p108, A1

If you're inspired by Amsterdam's masterpiece-filled galleries, street art and canalscapes, the De Pijp branch of this venerable Dutch art-supply shop is a great place to pick up canvases, brushes, oils, watercolours, charcoals and more. (www.vanbeekart.nl; Stadhouderskade 62-65; ⏰1-6pm Mon, 9am-6pm Tue-Fri, 10am-5pm Sat; 🚊16/24 Stadhouderskade)

Explore

Oosterpark & Around

Oosterpark is one of Amsterdam's most culturally diverse neighbourhoods. It has seen only a small bit of gentrification, though things are starting to pick up. Even so, the area feels fresher and more uncharted than other parts of the city. The best sights are off the everyday tourist path: the Tropenmuseum's global ephemera, a Moroccan and Turkish enclave, and several urban-cool bars.

The Sights in a Day

☀ Spend the morning yodelling, sitting in yurts and checking out Dutch colonial booty at the **Tropenmuseum** (p120; pictured opposite). Strike out east from here down 1e van Swindenstraat to find the **Dappermarkt** (p120), a fun cultural mix of people, food and wares mingling in the open air.

☼ Continue east and the road eventually turns into Javastraat, where old Dutch fish shops and working-class bars sit adjacent to Moroccan and Turkish grocery stores. The exotic strip offers prime grazing; sweet tooths will appreciate the divine bakeries. Assuming you're still hungry, keep going and you'll run into Javaplein for lunch at rustic **Wilde Zwijne** (p120). Or chill out nearby at the cafe of **Studio K** (p123).

☽ Dinner in the greenhouse at **De Kas** (p120) is a one-of-a-kind meal; reserve ahead. Options abound for an evening drink: great views and clubby goings-on at **Canvas** (p122), or burgers and beer in the garden at **De Biertuin** (p123). Then again, you could always fritter away the night watching boats float on the Amstel at **De Ysbreeker** (p122).

♥ **Best of Amsterdam**

Eating
De Kas (p120)
Roopram Roti (p122)

Canals
De Ysbreeker (p122)

Museums & Galleries
Tropenmuseum (p120)

Parks & Gardens
Oosterpark (p122)

Getting There

🚋 **Tram** Tram 9 goes from the city centre to the Tropenmuseum. Trams 10 and 14 swing through on their east–west routes, as well.

Ⓜ **Metro** The Wibautstraat stop is a stone's throw from the mod bars at the Oost's southwest edge.

A **B** **C** **D**

Nieuwe Keizersgracht

PLANTAGE

Plantage Middenlaan

Artis Royal Zoo

Sarphatistr

1

Nieuwe Kerkstr

Plantage Muidergracht

Westermanlaan

Alexanderplein

Nieuwe Prinsengr

Roetersstr

Alexanderkade

Nieuwe Achtergracht

Nieuwe Achtergr

Valckenierstr

Weesperstr

Tropenmuseum

◉ **1**

Valckenierstr

Spinozastr

Mauritskade

2

Valckenierstr

Sarphatistr

Ⓜ **Weesperplein**

Sajetplein

Muidendamstr

M Zeldenruststr

Mauritskade

Rhijnspoorplein

Oosterpark

De Schreeuv

Slavery Memorial

●

3

Weesperzijde

Ruysschstr

Onze Lieve Vrouwe Gasthuis

3.7

⊖**10**

2e Oosterparkstr

🅿**7**

Ruysschstraat

3e Oosterparkstr

1e Oosterparkstr

OOSTERPARKBUURT

Populierenweg

4

🍴**6**

Wibautstr

Amstel

Ⓜ **Wibautstraat**

Nobelweg

8⊖

Amsteldijk

GV Aemstelstr

5

3.

Mauritskade

Pieter Vlamingstr · Pontanusstr

Dapperstr

Von Zesenstr

Commellinstr

DAPPERBUURT

Wagenaarstr

9

1e Van Swindenstr · Dappermarkt ⊙2

5 · Dapperplein

2e Van Swindenstr

Pieter Nieuwlandstr

Reinwardstr

Wijttenbachstr

Linnaeusstr

Polderweg

Middenweg

Transvaalkade

TRANSVAALBUURT

59

Kamerlingh Onneslaan

12 ⊙ 3

Park Frankendael

Timorplein · ☆11 · Borneostr

Bankastr

Madurastr

Sumatrastr

Javastr

Balistr · **INDISCHE BUURT**

Celebesstr

1e Atjehstr · 1e Atjehstr

2e Atjehstr · Riaowstr

Insulindeweg

Molukkenstr · ☒4

Javaplein

🚉 Muiderpoort

Molukkenstr

22.65

15

Ⓝ 0 —————— 200 m
0 —————— 0.1 miles

For reviews see	
⊙ Sights	p120
☒ Eating	p120
⊟ Drinking	p122
☆ Entertainment	p123
Ⓐ Shopping	p123

Sights

Tropenmuseum
MUSEUM

1 ⊙ Map p118, D2

The Tropenmuseum houses a three-storey collection of colonial artefacts, presented with insight, imagination and a fair amount of multimedia. You can stroll through an African market or sit in a Central Asian yurt (traditional felt hut), see ritual masks and spiky spears and listen to recordings of exotic musical instruments. There's a children's section, a great gift shop and a cafe serving global foods. (Tropics Museum; ☑0880 042 800; www.tropenmuseum.nl; Linnaeusstraat 2; adult/child €12.50/8; ☺10am-5pm Tue-Sun; ☝; ☒9/10/14 Alexanderplein)

Dappermarkt
MARKET

2 ⊙ Map p118, E2

The larger Albert Cuypmarkt in De Pijp may be the king of street bazaars, but the Dappermarkt is a worthy prince. Reflecting the Oost's diverse immigrant population, it's a whirl of people (Africans, Turks, Dutch), foods (apricots, olives, fish) and goods from sports socks and shimmering fabrics to sunflowers, all sold from stalls lining the street. (www.dappermarkt.nl; Dapperstraat, btwn Mauritskade & Wijtenbachstraat; ☺9am-5pm Mon-Sat; ☒3/7 Dapperstraat)

Eating

De Kas
INTERNATIONAL €€€

3 ✖ Map p118, F5

Admired by gourmets citywide, De Kas has an organic attitude to match its chic glass greenhouse setting – try to visit during a thunderstorm! It grows most of its own herbs and produce right here and the result is incredibly pure flavours with innovative combinations. There's one set menu each day, based on whatever has been freshly harvested. Reserve in advance. (☑462 45 62; www.restaurantdekas.nl; Kamerlingh Onneslaan 3, Park Frankendael; lunch/dinner menu €39/49.50; ☺noon-2pm & 6.30-10pm Mon-Fri, 6.30-10pm Sat; ☑; ☒9 Hogeweg)

Wilde Zwijnen
MODERN DUTCH €€

4 ✖ Map p118, H1

The name means 'wild boar' and if it's the right time of year, you may indeed find it on the menu. The rustic, wood-tabled restaurant serves locally sourced, seasonal fare with bold results. There's usually a vegetarian option and chocolate ganache for dessert. The *eetbar* next door offers small plates for €7 to €12 if you don't want a full-on meal. (☑463 30 43; www.wildezwijnen.com; Javaplein 23; mains €19-22, 3-/4-course menu €30.50/36.50; ☺6-10pm Mon-Thu, noon-4pm & 6-10pm Fri-Sun; ☏; ☒14 Javaplein)

Understand

Multiculturalism & Immigration Conflict

Global Population

Scratch that vision of a metropolis of 6ft-tall blond people. With nearly half of its population hailing from other countries, Amsterdam rivals much bigger cities for diversity. People from former colonies Indonesia and Suriname form the largest minority groups. The other notable groups are Turks and Moroccans, many second-generation. The first wave came over in the 1960s, when the government recruited migrant workers to bridge a labour gap. The remaining 170 or so nationalities recorded in the most recent census represent the rest of the globe.

Tensions

Since 2000, the Netherlands' historically tolerant policy toward migrants has been called into question. Pim Fortuyn, a right-wing politician, declared the country 'full' before being assassinated in 2002. Social tensions flared anew in 2004, when filmmaker Theo van Gogh – known for his anti-Muslim views – was shot and stabbed to death on a street by Oosterpark. In a city famous for its open-mindedness, what did it mean that a native Amsterdammer, albeit of foreign descent, was behind the crime? The national government responded in 2006 by passing a controversial immigration law requiring newcomers to have competency in Dutch language and culture before they could get a residency permit. Citizens from the EU, USA and Japan were exempt due to pre-existing arrangements. This meant the policy mostly fell on immigrants from non-Western countries, including Morocco and Turkey.

Going Forward

While the national government swings more to the right and has tried to curb immigration, Amsterdam still leans left. It is quite integrated compared with many other European capitals. Immigrants aren't relegated to suburbs; just walk around De Pijp and you'll hear five or 10 languages spoken. The city's multiracial character is a point of pride, and post-Theo, many Amsterdammers have scoffed at nationalist politicians such as MP Geert Wilders, the firebrand who likened the Koran to *Mein Kampf*. And Amsterdammers always seem ready to bond over commerce – see the wildly diverse Albert Cuypmarkt in De Pijp and Dappermarkt in the Oost.

Roopram Roti

SURINAMESE €

5 🍴 Map p118, E2

There's often a line to the door at this bare-bones Surinamese place, but don't worry – it moves fast. Place your order – lamb roti 'extra' (with egg) and a *barra* (lentil doughnut) at least – at the bar and don't forget the fiery hot sauce. It's some of the flakiest roti you'll find anywhere. (1e Van Swindenstraat 4; mains €4-10; 🕑2-9pm Tue-Sun; 🚊9 1e Van Swindenstraat)

Eetcafe Ibis

ETHIOPIAN €€

6 🍴 Map p118, A4

African art and textiles decorate Ibis' wee room, a delightful spot to get your hands on (literally, using the spongy Ethiopian injera bread) herb-laced vegetable stews and spicy lamb and beef dishes. Ibis also sells African beers to accompany the authentic food. (📞692 62 67; www.eetcafeibis.com; Weesperzijde 43; mains €12-15; 🕑5-10pm Tue-Sun; 🍴; 🚊3 Wibautstraat/Ruyschstraat)

Drinking

De Ysbreeker

BROWN CAFÉ

7 🍺 Map p118, A3

The terrace at this *café* on the Amstel is glorious for watching the river lined with houseboats and other vessels gliding by. Inside, stylish drinkers hoist beverages in the plush booths and along the marble bar. It's great for organic and local beers (such as de Prael) and bar snacks such as lamb meatballs. (www.deysbreeker.nl; Weesperzijde 23; 🕑8am-1am Sun-Thu, to 2am Fri & Sat; 🛜; 🚊3 Wibautstraat/Ruyschstraat)

Canvas

BAR

8 🍺 Map p118, B5

Take the elevator to the 7th floor for this bar-club-restaurant atop the mod Volkshotel (located in the former *Volkskrant* newspaper office). Young creatives flock in for terrific views and cocktails in the edgy, urban-cool space. On weekend nights, it morphs into a fresh-beat dance club. Feeling wild? Sneak up to the roof for a dip in one of the hot tubs. (www.canvas7.nl; Wibautstraat 150;

🔍 Local Life
Oosterpark

Oosterpark (🕑dawn-dusk; 👣; 🚊9 1e Van Swindenstraat) was laid out in 1891 to accommodate the diamond traders who made their fortunes in the South African mines, and it still has an elegant, rambling feel, complete with regal grey herons swooping around the ponds. On the south side, look for two monuments: one commemorates the abolition of slavery in the Netherlands in 1863; the other, *De Schreeuw* (The Scream), honours free speech and, more specifically, filmmaker Theo van Gogh, who was murdered here in 2004.

⏱7am-1am Mon-Thu, to 4am Fri, 8am 4am Sat, to 1am Sun; Ⓜ Wibautstraat)

De Biertuin
BEER GARDEN

9 🍺 Map p118, E2

The name translates to 'the beer garden', and it is indeed the main feature. A young and beautiful crowd packs the beloved terrace (heated when the weather gets chilly). They bite into top-notch burgers and swill from the lengthy beer list (around 12 on tap and 50 more Dutch and Belgian varieties in the bottle). It's a big after-work hang-out. (www.debiertuin.nl; Linnaeusstraat 29; ⏱11am-1am Sun-Thu, to 3am Fri & Sat; 🛜; 🚊9 1e Van Swindenstraat)

Bar Bukowski
BAR

10 🍺 Map p118, C3

Named after the barfly writer Charles Bukowski, this art-deco *café* is a fine spot to channel the drinking and writing muse. Linger all day over a coffee, Heineken, banana milkshake or jasmine tea. Supplement with a baguette sandwich or *flammkuchen* (Alsatian thin-crust pizza). If you're looking for a stiffer drink, the owners have a cocktail bar next door (open Thursday, Friday and Saturday). (📞370 16 85; www.barbukowski.nl; Oosterpark 10; ⏱8am-1am Mon-Thu, to 3am Fri, 9am-3am Sat, to 1am Sun; 🚊3/7 Beukenweg)

Entertainment

Studio K
CINEMA, LIVE MUSIC

11 ⭐ Map p118, G1

Sporting two cinemas, a club, a stage for bands and theatre, an eclectic restaurant (serving sandwiches for lunch, and vegetarian-friendly, international-flavoured dishes for dinner) and a huge terrace, the student-run Studio K is your one-stop shop for hip culture in the Oost. Stop in for a coffee and you might wind up staying all night to dance. (📞692 04 22; www.studio-k.nu; Timorplein 62; ⏱11am-1am Sun-Thu, to 3am Fri & Sat; 🛜; 🚊14 Zeeburgerdijk)

Shopping

De Pure Markt
MARKET

12 🔒 Map p118, F5

On the last Sunday of the month De Pure Markt sets up in Park Frankendael (near De Kas restaurant), with stalls selling artisanal food and craft producers selling sausages, home-grown grapes and much more. Keep an eye out to the market's west for the community of garden plots with wee houses on them. (www.puremarkt.nl; Park Frankendael; ⏱11am-6pm Sun Mar-Oct & Dec; 🚊9 Hogeweg)

Nieuwmarkt & Plantage

Nieuwmarkt is a district as historic as anything you'll find in Amsterdam. Rembrandt painted canalscapes here, and Jewish merchants generated a fair share of the city's wealth with diamonds and other ventures. Affluent residents laid out the Plantage as a leafy, strollable quarter next door. The green area now hosts the botanic garden, zoo, inspiring resistance museum and a nifty windmill.

The Sights in a Day

☼ Begin at **Museum het Rembrandthuis** (p126), the master's impressive home where he painted his finest works. Nearby **Gassan Diamonds** (p132) gives the bling low-down via free factory tours. Those who prefer history to baubles can visit the **Joods Historisch Museum** (p132), which provides the backstory to the neighbourhood's role as the old Jewish quarter.

☼ Nosh on a hot-spiced Surinamese sandwich at **Tokoman** (p135), then spend the afternoon taking in the Plantage's many sights. The **Artis Royal Zoo** (p132) wows the kids. The time-hewn plants of the **Hortus Botanicus** (p133) and the resistance exhibits of the **Verzetsmuseum** (p132) impress all ages. When happy hour rolls around, stroll over to organic beermaker **Brouwerij 't IJ** (p137) and swill at the foot of an authentic windmill.

☾ Fork into contemporary Dutch cuisine at **Greetje** (p135) or **Gebr Hartering** (p135) for dinner. Then take your pick of the *cafés* around Nieuwmarkt square or head down the road to **Café de Doelen** (p137) for a nightcap.

For a local's day in Nieuwmarkt & Plantage, see p128.

◉ Top Sights

Museum het Rembrandthuis (p126)

◯ Local Life

Café-Hopping in Nieuwmarkt & Plantage (p128)

♥ Best of Amsterdam

Museums & Galleries
Verzetsmuseum (p132)

De Appel (p129)

Eating
Greetje (p135)

Tokoman (p135)

Drinking & Nightlife
Brouwerij 't IJ (p137)

De Sluyswacht (p129)

Getting There

🚊 **Tram** Trams 9 and 14 go to Waterlooplein, the Jewish sights and onward to the Plantage. Trams do not go to Nieuwmarkt square, but it's a short walk from Waterlooplein.

Ⓜ **Metro** There's a stop at Nieuwmarkt, though it's easier to tram to Waterlooplein and walk to the square.

Top Sights
Museum het Rembrandthuis

You almost expect to find the master himself at Museum het Rembrandthuis, set in the three-storey canal house where Rembrandt van Rijn lived and ran the Netherlands' largest painting studio between 1639 and 1658. He bought the abode at the height of his career, when he was awarded the prestigious *Night Watch* commission. The atmospheric, tchotchke-packed interior gives a real-deal feel for how Rembrandt painted his days away.

Rembrandt House Museum

Map p130, B3

520 04 00

www.rembrandthuis.nl

Jodenbreestraat 4

adult/child €12.50/4

10am-6pm

9/14 Waterlooplein

Museum het Rembrandthuis

Don't Miss

The House

The house dates from 1606. Rembrandt bought it for a fortune in 1639, made possible by his wealthy wife, Saskia van Uylenburgh. On the ground floor you'll see Rembrandt's living room/bedroom and the anteroom where he entertained clients.

Studio & Cabinet

Climb the narrow staircase and you'll come to Rembrandt's light-filled studio, laid out as though he's just nipped down to the kitchen for a bite to eat. Artists give demonstrations here on how Rembrandt sourced and mixed paints. Across the hall is Rembrandt's 'cabinet' – a mind-blowing room crammed with the curiosities he collected: seashells, glassware, Roman busts and stuffed alligators.

Etchings

The top floor is devoted to Rembrandt's famous etchings. The museum has a near-complete collection of them (about 250), although they're not all on display at once. Expect to see between 20 and 100 inky works at any one time, depending on the exhibition. Demonstrators crank up an oak press to show etching techniques several times daily.

Bankruptcy

The house ultimately caused Rembrandt's financial downfall. He was unable to pay off the mortgage, and in 1656 the household effects, artworks and curiosities were sold to compensate his creditors. It's thanks to the debt collector's itemised list that the museum has been able to reproduce the interior so authentically. Rembrandt lived the rest of his years in cheaper digs in the Jordaan.

☑ Top Tips

▶ Crowds are lightest right at opening time or after 3pm.

▶ You can buy advance tickets online, though it's not as vital here as at some of the other big museums.

▶ Pick up the free audio guide. It's available down the stairs past the entrance desk.

✕ Take a Break

Tables splash out of mosaic-trimmed **Tisfris** (Map p130, B3; www.tisfris. nl; St Antoniebreestraat 142; dishes €5-14; ◷ 9am 7pm; 🚊 9/14 Waterlooplein) and over the canal, almost to Rembrandthuis' door. Pull up a chair and ask about the sandwich of the day.

Behind the museum, food vendors waft falafel sandwiches, *frites* and other quick bites around the periphery of Waterlooplein Flea Market (p129).

Local Life
Café-Hopping in Nieuwmarkt & Plantage

Thanks to Nieuwmarkt's action-packed plaza and the Plantage's garden-district greenery, the area makes for lively and lovely strolling. Distinctive *cafés* are the bonus here: they pop up in rustic shipping warehouses, 17th-century lock-keeper's quarters, the turreted city gate, and just about everywhere in between. A flea market and funky arts centre add to the daily buzz.

❶ Fuel Up at Café Scharrebier

Join locals reading the newspaper and playing Scrabble at **Café Scharrebier** (scharrebier.nl; Rapenburgerplein 1; ⏲11am-1am Sun-Thu, to 3am Fri & Sat; 🚌22 Kadijksplein). Overlooking the lock, the terrace at this snug little brown *café* (traditional pub) is an inviting spot for a beer or sandwich. (Scharrebier, incidentally, was beer mixed with water to make it more affordable.)

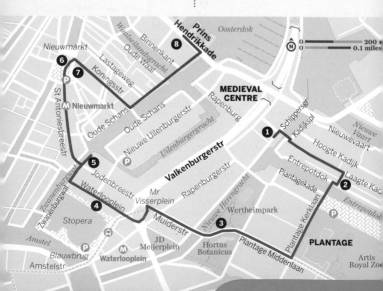

❷ Dockside at Entrepotdok

The Dutch East India Company, which grew rich on sea trade in the 17th century, owned **Entrepotdok** (🚆9/14 Plantage Kerklaan), a 500m row of warehouses that was the largest storage depot in Europe at the time. It's now packed with offices, apartments and dockside *cafés* perfect for lazing away a few hours at the water's edge.

❸ Wertheimpark's Memorial

Opposite the Hortus Botanicus, **Wertheimpark** (Plantage Parklaan; ⏰7am-9pm; 🚆9/14 Mr Visserplein) is a willow-shaded spot brilliant for lazing by the Nieuwe Herengracht. On the park's northeast side locals often place flowers at the Auschwitz Memorial, a panel of broken mirrors installed in the ground that reflects the sky.

❹ Flea Market Finds

Covering the square once known as Vlooienburg (Flea Town), the **Waterlooplein Flea Market** (www.waterlooplein markt.nl; Waterlooplein; ⏰9am-6pm Mon-Sat; 🚆9/14 Waterlooplein) draws sharp-eyed customers seeking everything from antique knick-knacks to designer knock-offs and cheap bicycle locks. The street market started in 1880 when local Jewish traders started selling their wares here.

❺ Beer at De Sluyswacht

Built in 1695, **De Sluyswacht** (www. sluyswacht.nl; Jodenbreestraat 1; ⏰12.30pm-1am Mon-Thu, to 3am Fri & Sat, to 7pm Sun; 🚆9/14 Waterlooplein) lists like a ship in a high wind. The tiny black building was once a lock-keeper's house on the Oude Schans. Today the canal-side terrace is one of the nicest spots in town to relax and down a Dutch beer (Dommelsch is the house speciality).

❻ The Multipurpose Waag

Dating from 1488, the ominous-looking **Waag** (www.indewaag.nl; Nieuwmarkt 4; Ⓜ Nieuwmarkt) was once a city gate, then a weigh house and now one of the many *cafés* that make surrounding Nieuwmarkt square a popular afternoon and evening hang-out. On Saturday a farmers market fills the plaza; on Sunday antiques take over.

❼ Fondue at Café Bern

Indulge in a dipping frenzy at delightfully well-worn **Café Bern** (📞622 00 34; www.cafebern.com; Nieuwmarkt 9; mains €12-18; ⏰kitchen 6-11pm Sep-Jun; Ⓜ Nieuwmarkt). Locals have been flocking here for more than 30 years for the Gruyère fondue and entrecôte (steak). The *café* closes for part of the summer, when steamy weather lessens the hot-cheese demand. Reservations advised.

❽ Art at De Appel

See what's on at the swanky contemporary-arts centre **De Appel** (📞625 56 51; www.deappel.nl; Prins Hendrikkade 142; adult/child €7/4.50; ⏰11am-6pm Tue-Sun; 🚆4/9/16/24 Centraal Station). The curators have a knack for tapping young international talent and supplementing exhibitions with lectures, film screenings and performances.

E | F | G | H

IJ Tunnel 32.39

NEMO

Naval Barracks

Dijksgracht

1

Historic Barges

Kattenburg

OOSTELIJKE EILANDEN

2

Het Scheepvaartmuseum

Kattenburgerstr

Wittenburg

42

Schippersgr

Kadijkspl

Nieuwevaart

Wittenburgergr

Kattenburgervaart

Grote Wittenburgerstr

Kleine Wittenburgerstr

3

Overhalsgang

Hoogte Kadijk

Oostenburgergr

Plantagekade

Laagte Kadijk

Entrepotdok

Entrepotdok

Nieuwe Vaart

4

age Parklaan

Verzetsmuseum

Henri Polaklaan

1 👁

Plantage Kerklaan

P

19 ✗
20 ♥

4 👁 Micropia

8 👁

PLANTAGE

3 👁 Artis Royal Zoo

Artis Royal Zoo

ollandsche chouwburg

Plantage Middenlaan

Plantage Muidergr

Plantage Muidergracht

Artis Aquarium & Artis Zoological Museum

Sarphatistr

5

Sights

Verzetsmuseum
MUSEUM

1 ◉ Map p130, E4

This museum shows, in no uncertain terms, how much courage it takes to actively resist an adversary so ruthless that you can't trust neighbours, friends, even family. Exhibits give an insight into the difficulties faced by those who fought the German occupation during WWII from within – as well as the minority who went along with the Nazis. Labels are in Dutch and English. Its **Verzetsmuseum Junior** relates the stories of four Dutch children, putting the resistance into context for kids. (Dutch Resistance Museum; ☎ 620 25 35; www.verzetsmuseum.org; Plantage Kerklaan 61; adult/child €10/5; ☃ 10am-5pm Tue-Fri, from 11am Sat-Mon; 🚋 9/14 Plantage Kerklaan)

Joods Historisch Museum
MUSEUM

2 ◉ Map p130, C4

The Joods Historisch Museum is a beautifully restored complex of four Ashkenazic synagogues from the 17th and 18th centuries. Displays show the rise of Jewish enterprise and the history of Jews in the Netherlands. The English-language audio tour is excellent (no extra charge). Tickets also include admission to the Portuguese-Israelite Synagogue (p133). (Jewish Historical Museum; ☎ 531 03 80; www.jhm.nl; Nieuwe Amstelstraat 1; adult/child €15/7.50; ☃ 11am-5pm; 🚋 9/14 Mr Visserplein)

Artis Royal Zoo
ZOO

3 ◉ Map p130, F5

Laid out with delightful ponds, statues and leafy, winding pathways, mainland Europe's oldest zoo has an alphabet soup of wildlife: alligators, birds, chimps and so on up to zebras. Highlights include convincing themed habitats like African savannah and tropical rainforest, and the aquarium complex featuring coral reefs, shark tanks and an Amsterdam canal displayed from a fish's point of view, plus a planetarium and kids' petting zoo. (☎ 523 34 00; www.artis.nl; Plantage Kerklaan 38-40; adult/child €19.95/16.50, incl Micropia €27/23; ☃ 9am-6pm Mar-Oct, to 5pm Nov-Feb; 🚋 9/14 Plantage Kerklaan)

Micropia
MUSEUM

4 ◉ Map p130, E4

The invisible becomes visible at the world's first microbe museum, where exhibits teach you not only about these tiny life forms, but also about yourself (how many microbes live on your body, what they do, and what can be learnt from them). It's especially aimed at getting kids interested in science. Ideal for ages eight and up. (www.micropia.nl; Artisplein, Plantage Kerklaan 38-40; adult/child €14/12, incl Artis Royal Zoo €27/23; ☃ 9am-6pm Sun-Wed, to 8pm Thu-Sat; 🚋 9/14 Artis)

Gassan Diamonds
FACTORY

5 ◉ Map p130, C3

At this vast workshop, you'll get a quick primer in assessing the gems for qual-

Hortus Botanicus

ity, and see diamond cutters and polishers in action. The one-hour tour is the best of its kind in town. The factory sits on Uilenburg, one of the rectangular islands reclaimed in the 1580s during a sudden influx of Sephardic Jews from Spain and Portugal. In the 1880s Gassan became the first diamond factory to use steam power. (www.gassan.com; Nieuwe Uilenburgerstraat 173-175; admission free; ⊙9am-5pm; 🚃9/14 Waterlooplein)

Hortus Botanicus   GARDENS
6 ⊙ Map p130, D4

Established in 1638, this venerable garden became a repository for tropical seeds and plants brought in (read: smuggled out of other countries) by

Dutch trading ships. From here, coffee, pineapple, cinnamon and palm-oil plants were distributed throughout the world. The 4000-plus species are kept in wonderful structures, including the colonial-era seed house and a three-climate glasshouse. (Botanical Garden; www.dehortus.nl; Plantage Middenlaan 2a; adult/child €8.50/4.50; ⊙10am-5pm daily, to 7pm Sun Jul & Aug; 🚃9/14 Mr Visserplein)

Portuguese-Israelite Synagogue   SYNAGOGUE
7 ⊙ Map p130, C4

This was the largest synagogue in Europe when it was completed in 1675, and it's still in use today. The interior features massive pillars and some two

Understand
Tilted Architecture

No, you're not drunk... Amsterdam's buildings *are* leaning. Some – like De Sluyswacht (p129) – have shifted over the centuries, but many canal houses were deliberately constructed to tip forward. Interior staircases were narrow, so owners needed an easy way to move large goods and furniture to the upper floors. The solution: a hoist built into the gable, to lift objects up and in through the windows. The tilt allows loading without bumping into the house front.

dozen brass candelabra. The library belonging to the Ets Haim seminary is one of the oldest and most important Jewish book collections in Europe. Outside (near the entrance) take the stairs underground to the treasure chambers to see 16th-century manuscripts and gold-threaded tapestries. Admission tickets also provide entry to the Joods Historisch Museum (p132). (www.portugesesynagoge.nl; Mr Visserplein 3; adult/child €15/7.50; ⏰10am-5pm Sun-Thu, to 4pm Fri, closed Sat Mar-Oct, reduced hours Nov-Feb; 🚊9/14 Mr Visserplein)

Hollandsche Schouwburg   MEMORIAL

8 🎯 Map p130, E5

This historic theatre – first known as the Artis Theatre after its inception in 1892 – quickly became a hub of cultural life in Amsterdam, staging major dramas and operettas. In WWII the occupying Germans turned it into a Jewish theatre, then, tragically, a detention centre for Jews held for deportation. (Holland Theatre; 📞531 03 10; www.hollandscheschouwburg.nl; Plantage Middenlaan 24; suggested donation €3; ⏰11am-5pm; 🚊9/14 Plantage Kerklaan)

Zuiderkerk   CHURCH

9 🎯 Map p130, B3

Dutch Renaissance architect Hendrick de Keyser built the 'Southern Church' in 1611. This was the first custom-built Protestant church in Amsterdam – still Catholic in design but with no choir. The final church service was held here in 1929. During the 'Hunger Winter' of WWII it served as a morgue. The interior is now used for private events, but you can tour the tower once it reopens after renovations in 2017 for a sky-high city view. (zuiderkerkamsterdam. nl; Zuiderkerkhof 72; Ⓜ Nieuwmarkt)

Scheepvaarthuis   ARCHITECTURE

10 🎯 Map p130, C1

Now the luxury Grand Hotel Amrath, the grand 1916-built Scheepvaarthuis was the first true example of Amsterdam School architecture. The exterior resembles a ship's bow and is encrusted in elaborate detailing; look for figures of Neptune, his wife and four females that represent the compass points. Step inside to admire stained glass, light fixtures and the art-deco-ish central stairwell. (Shipping House; Prins Hendrikkade 108; 🚊4/9/16/24 Centraal Station)

Eating

Greetje
MODERN DUTCH €€€

11 🍴 Map p130, D3

Using market-fresh organic produce, Greetje resurrects and recreates traditional Dutch recipes like pickled beef, braised veal with apricots and leek *stamppot* (traditional mashed potatoes and vegetables), and pork belly with Dutch mustard sauce. A good place to start is the two-person Big Beginning (per person €15), with a sampling of hot and cold starters. (☎779 74 50; www.restaurantgreetje.nl; Peperstraat 23-25; mains €23-27; ⏰6-10pm Sun-Fri, to 11pm Sat; 🚌22/34/35/48 Prins Hendrikkade)

Gebr Hartering
MODERN DUTCH €€

12 🍴 Map p130, D2

At this jewel of a restaurant founded by two brothers, the menu changes daily so you never know what you'll be tasting, but dishes are unfailingly delicious and exquisitely presented. The wine list is succinct and the timber dining room and canal-side location impossibly romantic. (☎421 06 99; www.gebr-hartering.nl; Peperstraat 10; 4-/7-course menu €40/65 Tue, Wed & Sun, 6-/9-course menu €50/75 Thu-Sat; ⏰6-10.30pm Tue-Sun; 🚌32/33 Prins Hendrikkade)

Sterk Staaltje
DELI €

13 🍴 Map p130, A4

From the fruit stacked up in crates on the pavement, Sterk Staaltje looks like an unassuming greengrocer's, but inside it's a veritable treasure chest of ready-to-eat treats: teriyaki meatballs, feta and sundried tomato quiche, pumpkin-stuffed wraps, a soup of the day, and fantastic sandwiches (roast beef, horseradish and rocket; marinated chicken with guacamole and sour cream) plus salads and pastas. (sterkstaaltje.com; Staalstraat 12; dishes €4-7.60; ⏰8am-7pm Mon-Fri, 8am-6pm Sat, 11am-5pm Sun; 🚌4/9/14/16/24 Muntplein)

Moes
MODERN DUTCH €€

14 🍴 Map p130, D2

The bar-restaurant in the basement of De Appel arts centre (p129) has a farm-to-fork credo. There's always a fish of the day and a daily vegetarian special made with local ingredients. Mains vary, but might include kohlrabi ravioli with peas and mint, or slow-cooked pork neck with borlotti beans. A fine selection of organic

---

🔍 Local Life
Tokoman

Queue with the folks getting their Surinamese spice on at **Tokoman** (Waterlooplein 327; sandwiches €3-4.50, dishes €6.50-12.50; ⏰11am-8pm Mon-Sat; 🚌9/14 Waterlooplein). Chowhounds agree it makes the best *broodje pom* (a sandwich filled with a tasty mash of chicken and a starchy tuber). You'll want the *zuur* (pickled-cabbage relish) and *peper* (chilli) on it, plus a cold can of coconut water.

wines and ciders adds to the scrumptiousness. (📞623 54 77; www.totmoes.nl; Prins Hendrikkade 142; mains €11.50-19.50; 🕐5-11pm Tue-Fri, 11am-11pm Sat, 11am-6pm Sun; 🥗; 🚊4/9/16/24 Centraal Station)

Hemelse Modder MODERN DUTCH €€

15 Map p130, C2

Celery-green walls and blond-wood tables are the backdrop for equally light and unpretentious food, which emphasises North Sea fish and farm-fresh produce in dishes like roast guinea fowl with porcini and morel sauce, followed by desserts like luscious berry pudding and namesake *hemelse modder* (heavenly mud) dark-and white-chocolate mousse. The back terrace makes for lovely al fresco dining. (📞624 32 03; www.hemelsemodder. nl; Oude Waal 11; mains €20, 3-course menu €35; 🕐6-11pm; Ⓜ Nieuwmarkt)

Local Life
The Green Elephant

Steeped in Victorian-era opulence with intricate woodwork, **De Groene Olifant** (www.degroeneolifant. nl; Sarphatistraat 510; 11am-1am Sun-Thu, to 2am Fri & Sat; 🚊9 Alexanderplein) transports you back in time. Sit at the circa-1880 bar with the locals and admire the art-deco glass, or retreat to the lofted dining room for dinner like the the elegant residents of yesteryear's Plantage.

Toko Joyce INDONESIAN €

16 Map p130, B2

Pick and mix a platter of Indonesian-Surinamese food from the glass case. The 'lunch box' (you choose noodles or rice, plus two spicy, coconutty toppings) is good value. To finish, get a wedge of *spekkoek* (moist, layered gingerbread). Take your meal upstairs to the handful of tables, or head outside where canal-side benches beckon a few steps from the door. (www.tokojoyce.nl; Nieuwmarkt 38; dishes €6.50-10.50; 🕐4-8pm Mon, from 11am Tue-Sat, from 1pm Sun; Ⓜ Nieuwmarkt)

Frenzi MEDITERRANEAN €€

17 Map p130, A4

Stunning tapas at this casual spot will sate your hunger – Manchego cheese and fig compote; marinated sardines; portobello mushrooms with melted Gorgonzola – but save room for mains: pan-fried cod with fennel mash, pumpkin gnocchi with wilted spinach, or leg of lamb with roast asparagus. It stocks 110 types of grappa; live jazz plays on Saturdays at 3pm. (📞423 51 12; www. frenzi-restaurant.nl; Zwanenburgwal 232; mains lunch €7-14, dinner €14.50-18.50, tapas €4.50-6; 🕐11am-10pm; 🚊4/9/14/16/24 Muntplein)

Latei CAFE €€

18 Map p130, B2

Young locals throng groovy Latei, where you can buy the lamps (or any of the vintage decor) right off the wall. The split-level cafe does unusual dinners Thursday through Saturday, often an Ethiopian, Indian or Indonesian dish by the local 'cooking collective'. Otherwise it serves sandwiches, apple pie and *koffie verkeerd* (milky coffee). A cat named Elvis roams the premises. (www.latei.net; Zeedijk 143; lunch dishes €3.75-6.50, dinner mains €6-16, ⏰8am-6pm Mon-Wed, to 10pm Thu & Fri, 9am-10pm Sat, 11am-6pm Sun; 🖉; Ⓜ Nieuwmarkt)

IJsmolen
ICE CREAM €

19 ❌ Map p130, H4

Homemade ice cream at this spot near the De Gooyer windmill comes in Dutch flavours like *stroopwafel* (classic caramel-syrup-filled wafers) and *speculaas* (spicy Christmas biscuits) as well as mango and mint; *stracciatella* (vanilla with shredded chocolate); watermelon; and lemon cheesecake. On hot days it stays open to 10pm. (Zeeburgerstraat 2; 1/2/4 scoops €1.50/2.75/4.75; ⏰noon-9pm; 🚋10 Hoogte Kadijk)

Drinking

Brouwerij 't IJ
BREWERY

20 🚇 Map p130, H4

Beneath the creaking sails of the 1725-built De Gooyer windmill, Amsterdam's leading organic microbrewery produces delicious (and often very potent) standard, seasonal and limited-edition brews. Pop in for a beer in the tiled tasting room, lined by an amazing bottle collection, or on the plane-tree-shaded terrace. A beer is included in the 30-minute brewery tour

(€4.50). (www.brouwerijhetij.nl; Funenkade 7; ⏰brewery 2-8pm, English tour 3.30pm Fri-Sun; 🚋10 Hoogte Kadijk)

Café de Doelen
BROWN CAFÉ

21 🚇 Map p130, A4

Set on a busy canal-side crossroad between the Amstel and the Red Light District, De Doelen dates back to 1895 and looks it: there's a carved wooden goat's head, stained-glass lamps, and sand on the floor. In fine weather the tables spill across the street for picture-perfect canal views. (Kloveniersburgwal 125; ⏰9am-1am Mon-Thu, 9am-3am Fri & Sat, 10am-1am Sun; 🚋4/9/14/16/24 Muntplein)

Cafe de Engelbewaarder
BROWN CAFÉ

22 🚇 Map p130, A3

Jazz fans will want to settle in at this little *café* on Sunday afternoon from 4.30pm September to June for an open session that has earned quite a following. The rest of the time, it's a tranquil place to sip a beer (there are 15 on tap) by the sunny windows. (www.cafe-de-engelbewaarder.nl; Kloveniersburgwal 59; ⏰10am-1am Mon-Fri, 10am-3am Fri & Sat, noon-1am Sun; Ⓜ Nieuwmarkt)

Bluebird
COFFEESHOP

23 🚇 Map p130, B3

Away from Nieuwmarkt's main cluster of coffeeshops, Bluebird has a less touristy, more local vibe. The space has beautiful murals and local artists' paintings, lounge with leather chairs, non-alcoholic bar and kitchen serving superior snacks such as freshly made pancakes. It's especially well known for its hash, including varieties unavailable elsewhere in Amsterdam. (Sint Antoniesbreestraat 71; ⏱9.30am-1am; Ⓜ Nieuwmarkt)

Entertainment

Muziektheater
CLASSICAL MUSIC

24 ⭐ Map p130, B4

The Muziektheater is home to the Netherlands Opera and the National Ballet. Big-name performers and international dance troupes also take the stage here. Visitors aged under 30 can get tickets for €10 to €15 by showing up 90 minutes before show time. Free classical concerts (12.30pm to 1pm) are held most Tuesdays from September to May in its Boekmanzaal. (☎625 54 55; www.operaballet.nl; Waterlooplein 22; ⏱box office noon-6pm Mon-Fr, to 3pm Sat & Sun or until performance Sep-Jul; 🚊9/14 Waterlooplein)

Bethaniënklooster
CLASSICAL MUSIC

25 ⭐ Map p130, A2

This former monastery near Nieuwmarkt has a glorious ballroom, and is a superb place to take in exceptional chamber music. Jazz fills the vaulted basement cellar. Concert schedules are online. (☎625 00 78; www.bethanien klooster.nl; Barndesteeg 6b; ⏱Sep-Jul; Ⓜ Nieuwmarkt)

Shopping

Droog
DESIGN, HOMEWARES

26 🔒 Map p130, A4

Droog means 'dry' in Dutch, and this slick local design house's products are strong on dry wit. You'll find all kinds of smart items you never knew you needed, like super-powerful suction cups. Also here is a gallery space, whimsical blue-and-white cafe, and fairytale-inspired courtyard garden that Alice in Wonderland would love, as well as a top-floor apartment (double €275). (www.droog.com; Staalstraat 7; ⏱11am-6pm Tue-Sun; 🚊4/9/14/16/24 Muntplein)

Knuffels
TOYS, SHOES

27 🔒 Map p130, B3

Kids will be drawn to the bobbing mobiles hanging from the ceiling of this busy corner shop, as wells as the *knuffels* (soft cuddly toys), puppets, teddies and jigsaw puzzles. As a bonus, there's a clog shop downstairs with wooden shoes galore. (www.knuffels.com; St Antoniesbreestraat 39-51; ⏱10am-6pm Mon-Sat, from 11am Sun; 👶; Ⓜ Nieuwmarkt)

Het Fort van Sjakoo
BOOKS

28 🔒 Map p130, B4

Get the low-down on the squat scene, plus locally produced zines and Trotsky translations, at this lefty bookshop, which has been in operation since 1977. (☎625 89 79; www.sjakoo. nl; Jodenbreestraat 24; ⏱11am-6pm Mon-Fri, to 5pm Sat; 🚊9/14 Waterlooplein)

Droog

Henxs
CLOTHING

29 Map p130, B3

The two tiny floors of this indie clothes store are crammed with fave labels of skaters and graffiti artists, such as Hardcore, Bombers Best, Evisu and G-Star. Graffiti supplies and edgy accessories are available in Henxs' space next door. (www.henxs.com; St Antoniesbreestraat 136-138; ☺11am-6pm Mon-Fri, to 5pm Sat; M Nieuwmarkt)

Juggle
CIRCUS SUPPLIES

Just around the corner from Café De Doelen (see **21** Map p130, A4), Juggle puts more than mere balls in the air: it also sells circus supplies, from unicycles to fire hoops to magic tricks. (www.juggle-store.com; Staalstraat 3; ☺noon-5.30pm Tue-Sat; 4/9/14/16/24 Muntplein)

Marbles Vintage
CLOTHING

30 Map p130, A4

Pretty, feminine and reasonably priced, Marbles offers a wonderfully curated selection of vintage skirts, dresses, coats, shoes, boots and jewellery. Items are sorted by colour and type. Clothes hounds can launch from here into several other hip new and secondhand clothing stores on the same block. There are branches in Jordaan and De Pijp. (Staalstraat 30; ☺11am-7pm; 4/9/14/16/24 Muntplein)

Explore

Harbour & Eastern Islands

The former shipyard and warehouse district that was once the city's fringe has morphed into a hub for cutting-edge Dutch architecture. The sparkling Muziekgebouw aan 't IJ and terrific maritime museum beguile, but mostly a visit here is about gawping at innovative structures. A scattering of bars and restaurants make the most of their dramatic waterfront locations.

The Sights in a Day

🔆 Tick off the main sights in the morning. Take the escalators to the top-floor cafe of the **Centrale Bibliotheek Amsterdam** (p144) for a great view of the cityscape (and optional breakfast). Walk over the bridge to wild-looking **NEMO** (p144; pictured opposite), Amsterdam's kiddie-mobbed science centre. Continue along the waterfront to **ARCAM** (p145) to stock up on architectural info. Then plunge into **Het Scheepvaartmuseum** (p144), the treasure-rich maritime museum.

🔆 Spend the afternoon exploring the Eastern Islands' odd, mod architecture. Pop into **De Wereldbol** (p146) for a sandwich to fortify. Then start wandering past buildings like the huge angular silver one dubbed the **Whale** (p145). Make your way to **Amsterdam Roest** (p147), where something hip is always going on at the artists' collective/beer garden. **Hannekes Boom** (p147) is another neighbourhood hang-out known for its awesome beer garden.

🌙 Reserve ahead for a sustainable seafood dinner at **Zouthaven** (p145). Follow with an evening of music. The big-gun **Muziekgebouw aan 't IJ** (p148), jazzy **Bimhuis** (p149) and lower-priced **Conservatorium van Amsterdam** (p149) play notes here.

💜 Best of Amsterdam

Museums & Galleries
Het Scheepvaartmuseum (p144)

For Kids
NEMO (p144)

Centrale Bibliotheek
Amsterdam (p144)

Entertainment
Muziekgebouw aan 't IJ (p148)

Bimhuis (p149)

Conservatorium
van Amsterdam (p149)

For Free
ARCAM (p145)

Getting There

🚋 **Tram** Tram 10 goes to the Eastern Islands by way of the Jordaan and Southern Canal Belt. Tram 26 goes from Centraal Station to the Muziekgebouw and the harbour's northeastern bits.

🚌 **Bus** Buses 22 and 48 (via Centraal Station) pick up the slack for areas that the tram doesn't reach.

A B C D

1

Het IJ

Javabrug

6 ✕ ☆ 18
☆ 19
Piet Heinkade
26

◉ *Passenger Terminal Amsterdam*

Vriesseveem

326

2

Oosterdoksstr
14 *Centrale Bibliotheek*
◉ *Amsterdam*
3 ◉ *32.39*
☆ 20 13
✕ *Oosterdoksdade*
9

Dijksgracht

Naval Barracks

Oosterdok

2 ◉ *NEMO*

3

22.48

Historic Barges

Kattenburg

Kattenburgerstr 42

Kattenburgervaart

Wittenburg

Oude Schans

MEDIEVAL CENTRE

ARCAM
◉ 4

1 ◉ *Het Scheepvaartmuseum*

Grote Wittenburgerstr
Kleine Wittenburgerstr

4

Uilenburgergracht

Valkenburgerstr

Schippersgr
Kadijkspl
Nieuwevaart

Nieuwe Vaart
Overhalsgang

Wittenburgerg

23 🔒

Oostenburg

Waalgat

Oostenburgerg

Piantagekade

Hoogte Kadijk

Entrepotdok

5

For reviews see	
◉ Sights	p144
✕ Eating	p145
🅟 Drinking	p147
☆ Entertainment	p148
🔒 Shopping	p149

🅟

PLANTAGE

Artis Royal Zoo

E F G H

0   500 m
0   0.25 miles

1

48
Java
Eiland Sumatrakade

Javakade

KNSM
Eiland Surinamekade
21 22
🔒 🔒 ✖10

EASTERN
DOCKLANDS 16 🚇 ✖8
Levantkade **2**

IJ Haven

🚇17

Veemkade

Oostelijke Handelskade

Lloydplein

🚇15

Rietlandpark

10

OOSTELIJKE
EILANDEN

🚇12

Oostenburg

Whale
◉
5 **3**

CJK van Aalststr

65 Panamakade

26 Piet Hein Tunnel 26

Borneolaan

4

Zeeburgerkade

11 ✖🚇 10

Conradst
Czaar Peterstr
Blankenstr

✖7 Cruquiusweg

5

Zeeburgerpad

14 Singelgracht

Zeeburgerdijk 22

Sights

Het Scheepvaartmuseum
MUSEUM

1 ◉ Map p142, B4

An immense, 17th-century admiralty building houses one of the world's most extensive collections of maritime memorabilia. Early shipping routes, naval combat, fishing and whaling are all detailed, and there are some 500 models of boats and ships. A full-scale replica of the Dutch East India Company's 700-tonne *Amsterdam*, one of the largest ships of the fleet, is moored outside. (Maritime Museum; ☏ 523 22 22; www.scheepvaartmuseum.nl; Kattenburgerplein 1; adult/child €15/7.50; ⊘ 9am-5pm; ☐ 22/48 Kattenburgerplein)

Understand
Eastern Islands' History

The Eastern Islands – Kattenburg, Wittenburg and Oostenburg – comprise the area around Het Scheepvaartmuseum. They were constructed in the 1650s to handle Amsterdam's rapidly expanding seaborne trade. The Dutch East India Company set itself up on Oostenburg, where it established warehouses, rope yards, workshops and docks for the maintenance of its fleet. Private shipyards and dockworkers' homes dominated the central island of Wittenburg. Admiralty offices and buildings arose on the westernmost island of Kattenburg, and warships were fitted out in the adjoining naval dockyards that are still in use today.

NEMO
MUSEUM

2 ◉ Map p142, B3

Perched atop the entrance to the IJ Tunnel is the science and technology museum, NEMO. The green-copper building rises from the waterfront like a ship setting sail. Its hands-on exhibits (with English explanations) are winners with kids and adults: drawing with a laser, 'antigravity' trick mirrors and a 'lab' for answering such questions as 'How black is black?' and 'How do you make cheese?'. NEMO's stepped, deck-like roof is the city's largest summer terrace with panoramic views. (☏ 531 32 33; www.e-nemo.nl; Oosterdok 2; admission €15, roof terrace free; ⊘ 10am-5.30pm, closed Mon Sep-Mar; ☐ 22/48 IJ-Tunnel)

Centrale Bibliotheek Amsterdam
LIBRARY

3 ◉ Map p142, A2

This nine-storey 'tower of knowledge' (its self-appointed nickname) is the country's largest library. Unveiled in 2007, it has claimed a commanding spot in Amsterdam's increasingly modern landscape. Inviting chairs and couches are scattered around, as are loads of free internet terminals (there's also free wi-fi). Panoramic city views unfold from the top-floor cafe. (Amsterdam Central Library; ☏ 523 09 00; www.

oba.nl; Oosterdokskade 143; admission free; ⏰10am-10pm; 🚊4/9/16/24/26 Centraal)

ARCAM ARCHITECTURE

4 🎯 Map p142, B4

This showpiece building of the Amsterdam Architecture Foundation is a one-stop shop for all your architectural needs. Expert staff are on hand to interpret the fascinating changing exhibits, and you can find books, guide maps and suggestions for tours on foot, by bike and by public transport. (Stichting Architectuurcentrum Amsterdam; 📞620 48 78; www.arcam.nl; Prins Hendrikkade 600; admission free; ⏰1-5pm Tue-Sat; 🚊22/48 Kadijksplein)

Whale ARCHITECTURE

5 🎯 Map p142, H3

Built between 1998 and 2000 by Dutch architect Frits van Dongen, this energy-efficient, zinc-clad apartment block has two raised corners to allow more natural light inside, resulting in its unique whale-like shape (best appreciated from Levantkade on KNSM Eiland). (Ertskade; 🚊10 JF Van Hengelstraat)

Eating

Zouthaven SEAFOOD €€

6 🍴 Map p142, B1

The Muziekgebouw aan 't IJ's flash dining space is hard to beat for location and views. Several storeys of glass and a sweeping terrace give you

☑️ Top Tip

Sightseeing from the Tram

Amsterdam's tram lines rattle through great cross-sections of the city and offer a terrific bit of passive sightseeing. Tram 10 is one of the most all-compassing routes. It starts near Westerpark, swings around the perimeter of the canal loop and heads out to the Eastern Islands, passing 19th-century housing blocks, the Rijksmuseum and Brouwerij 't IJ windmill along the way. Tram 2 is another good one, zipping from Centraal Station by the Dam, the canals, the Rijks and Van Gogh museums, and all along Vondelpark's southern edge.

an IJ's-eye perspective, and the food, such as a haddock and Zeeland mussels terrine or herb-crusted salmon, is superb. The seafood is sustainable and/or organic. (📞788 20 90; www.zouthaven.nl; Piet Heinkade 1, Muziekgebouw aan 't IJ; mains lunch €7.50-14.50, dinner €20-26.50; ⏰11.30am-10pm; 🚊26 Muziekgebouw)

Gare de l'Est INTERNATIONAL €€

7 🍴 Map p142, G5

You won't know what to expect from the four courses on the surprise menu until they arrive, but dietary requirements (including vegetarianism) can be accommodated. Portuguese tiles and glowing Middle Eastern lamps adorn the interior of the charming

1901 building, but in warm weather the best seats are in the courtyard. (463 06 20; www.garedelest.nl; Cruquiusweg 9; 4-course menu €33; 6-10pm; 22 Het Funen)

De Wereldbol INTERNATIONAL €€

8 Map p142, H2

A passionate and personable owner-chef, an ever-changing menu and an idyllic view of boats bobbing on the water make this small, dark-wood restaurant a fine place to stop for lunchtime soups, salads and sandwiches or end a day of sightseeing in the area dining on dishes like sea bass with squid-ink spaghetti and banana bread with homemade banana ice cream. (362 87 25; www.dewereldbol.nl; Piraeusplein 59; mains lunch €7.50-16, dinner €17.50-20.50, 3-course menu €35; noon-9pm Tue-Sun; 10 Azartplein)

Sea Palace CHINESE €€

9 Map p142, A3

It's a funny thing about floating Chinese restaurants: they look like tourist traps but so often serve superb food. The Sea Palace's three floors are busy with locals and visitors who aren't only here for the great views of the city from across the IJ. Try the incredible array of dim sum or the fiery hotpot. Reservations recommended. (626 47 77; www.seapalace.nl; Oosterdokskade 8; mains €17-38, dim sum €4-8.50; noon-11pm; 4/9/16/24/26 Centraal)

Kompaszaal CAFE €€

10 Map p142, H2

Set in the century-old Royal Dutch Steamboat Company (KNSM in Dutch) arrivals hall, this airy cafe has a breezy menu of dishes like lemon sole with artichokes and lavender butter, and roast poussin with aioli and Turkish *pilav* (buttery rice cooked in seasoned broth). Equally captivating are the groovy green tiles and the water view from the balcony. (419 95 96; www.kompaszaal.nl; KNSM-laan 311; mains lunch €6-13.50, dinner €15-21, high tea €17.50; kitchen 10am-5pm Wed, 10am-10pm Thu & Fri, 11am-10pm Sat & Sun; ; 10 Azartplein)

Instock INTERNATIONAL €€

11 Map p142, E5

Instock's raison d'être is reducing food waste. Its electric 'food rescue car' visits shops such as grocery chain Albert Heijn, Hilton Meats, fishmonger Jan van As, and Heineken to collect products that are still in date but would otherwise be thrown out. Instock then transforms them into delicious three-course meals (including a daily vegetarian option). Ingredients depending, prices can vary slightly. (www.instock.nl; Czaar Peterstraat 21; dishes €4-10, 3-course dinner menu €26; 9am-10pm Sun-Wed, to 11pm Thu-Sat; ; 10 Eerste Coehoornstraat)

ARCAM (p145)

Drinking

Amsterdam Roest · BEER GARDEN

12 · Map p142, E3

Derelict shipyards have been transformed into a super-cool artist collective/bar/restaurant, Amsterdam Roest (Dutch for 'Rust'), with a canal-facing terrace beneath towering blue cranes and an industrial warehouse interior. Regular events held here include films, live music, festivals and markets; there's a urban beach in summer and bonfires in winter. (www.amsterdamroest.nl; Jacob Bontiusplaats 1; ⏲11am-1am Sun-Thu, to 3pm Fri & Sat; 🚊22 Wittenburgergracht)

Hannekes Boom · BEER GARDEN

13 · Map p142, B2

Just across the water from NEMO, yet a local secret, this laidback waterside *café* built from recycled materials has a beer garden that really feels like a garden, with timber benches, picnic tables and summer barbecues. Mellow live music such as jazz or singer-songwriters takes place from 3.30pm on Sundays. (www.hannekesboom.nl; Dijksgracht 4; ⏲10am-1am Sun-Thu, to 3am Fri & Sat; 🚊26 Muziekgebouw)

(khl.nl; Oostelijke Handelskade 44; ⊘noon-midnight Tue-Sun; 🚊26 Rietlandpark)

Kanis & Meiland
BAR

16 🍸 Map p142, H2

A favourite among the 'islanders', this cavernous spot has an inviting wooden reading table, tall windows facing the 'mainland' and a quiet terrace directly on the water. (www.kanisenmeiland.nl; Levantkade 127; ⊘8.30am-1am Mon-Fri, 10am-1am Sat & Sun; 🛜; 🚊10 Azartplein)

Mezrab
CLUB

17 🍸 Map p142, E2

Well known for its hilariously fun hard-rock karaoke as well as its alternative dance nights, regular indie rock, jazz, world music and other live music gigs, this harbourside venue (formerly Café Pakhuis Wilhelmina) is low-key clubbing at its best. It also hosts storytelling sessions in English and Dutch on the last Thursday of the month. Hours can vary. Cash only. (☎419 33 68; www.mezrab.nl; Veemkade 576; ⊘8pm-1am Sun-Thu, to 3am Fri & Sat; 🚊26 Kattenburgerstraat)

Entertainment

Muziekgebouw aan 't IJ
CONCERT VENUE

18 ⭐ Map p142, B1

Behind this multidisciplinary performing-arts venue's hightech exterior, the dramatically lit main hall has a flexible stage layout and great

---

☑️ Top Tip
By Bike

Cycling is one of the best ways to explore the neighbourhood. The MacBike (www.macbike.nl) rental shop at Centraal Station is closest. From there it's a 10-minute pedal to the harbour and Eastern Islands. The shop also sells cycling maps that point out the area's architectural highlights.

SkyLounge
COCKTAIL BAR

14 🍸 Map p142, A2

An unrivalled 360-degree panorama of Amsterdam extends from the glass-walled SkyLounge on the 11th floor of the DoubleTree Amsterdam Centraal Station hotel – and just gets better when you head out to its vast, sofa-strewn SkyTerrace, with an outdoor bar. Deliberate over more than 500 different cocktails; DJs regularly hit the decks. (doubletree3.hilton.com; Oosterdoksstraat 4; ⊘11am-1am Sun-Thu, to 3am Fri & Sat; 🚊1/2/4/5/9/14/16/24 Centraal Station)

KHL
BAR

15 🍸 Map p142, G3

Set in a historic 1917 brick former warehouse with stunning tile work, KHL opens to a terrace that makes a superb spot for a glass of wine sourced from small vineyards. Regular live music ranges from Latin to pop and *klezmer* (traditional Jewish music).

acoustics. Its jazz stage, Bimhuis, is more intimate. Under-30s can get €10 tickets at the box office 30 minutes before show time. Everyone else should try the Last Minute Ticket Shop (p179) for discounts. (🎫 tickets 788 20 00; www.muziekgebouw.nl; Piet Heinkade 1; tickets free-€37; 🕐 box office noon-6pm Mon-Sat & 90min before performance; 🚊 26 Muziekgebouw)

Bimhuis   JAZZ

19 ⭐ Map p142, B2

Bimhuis is the beating jazz heart of the Netherlands, and its stylish digs at the Muziekgebouw aan 't IJ draw international jazz greats. (🎫 788 21 88; bimhuis.nl; Piet Heinkade 3; tickets free-€28; 🕐 closed Aug; 🚊 26 Muziekgebouw)

Conservatorium van Amsterdam   CLASSICAL MUSIC

20 ⭐ Map p142, A2

Catch a classical recital by students at the Netherlands' largest conservatory of music. It's in a snazzy contemporary building with state-of-the-art acoustics, endless glass walls and light-flooded interiors. (🎫 527 78 37; www.ahk.nl/conservatorium; Oosterdokskade 151; 🚊 4/9/16/24 Centraal Station)

Shopping

Loods 6   SHOPPING CENTRE

21 🛍 Map p142, H2

This isn't a shopping centre of the mall variety, but rather a string

of shops in a 1900-built former Royal Dutch Steam Company (KNSM) customs warehouse and passenger terminal. Noteworthy shops include children's wear designer **Imps & Elfs** (www.imps-elfs.com; KNSM-Laan 297, Loods 6; 🕐 10am-6pm Tue-Sat, noon-5pm Sun; 🚊 10 Azartplein), and Dutch-designed pottery and homewares at Pols Potten, as well as art galleries and fashion. (www.loods6.nl; KNSM-laan 143; 🚊 10 Azartplein)

Pols Potten   HOMEWARES

22 🛍 Map p142, H2

How do new residents in this style-conscious district furnish their new apartments? They head straight to this large interior-design shop, which has some particularly stunning ceramic work. (🎫 419 35 41; www.polspotten.nl; KNSM-laan 39, Loods 6; 🕐 10am-6pm Tue-Sat, noon-5pm Sun; 🚊 10 Azartplein)

Frank's Smokehouse   FOOD & DRINK

23 🛍 Map p142, D4

Frank is a prime supplier to Amsterdam's restaurants, and his excellent Alaskan salmon, halibut and yellowfin tuna can be vacuum-packed for travelling (customs regulations permitting). He also sells stunning sandwiches (smoked halibut with pumpkin relish; king crab; wild boar and cranberry chutney). (www.smokehouse.nl; Wittenburgergracht 303; 🕐 9am-4pm Mon, to 6pm Tue-Fri, to 5pm Sat; 🚊 22 Wittenburgergracht)

The Best of
Amsterdam

Traditional Dutch buildings
S.BORISOV / SHUTTERSTOCK ©

Best Walks
Amsterdam's Splashiest Canals

🏃 The Walk

Get the camera ready, because this walk passes some of the city's most beautiful waterways. They're more than just a pretty picture, though. For more than four centuries the canals have performed the epic task of keeping Amsterdam above water, since they help drain the soggy landscape. The romantic backdrops and groovy places to float a boat are a lucky bonus.

Start Corner of Staalstraat and Groenburgwal; 🚊 4/9/14/16/24 Muntplein

Finish De Ysbreeker; 🚊 3 Wibautstraat/Ruyschstraat

Length 3km; two hours with dawdling

✗ Take a Break

Sip coffee and enjoy the vintage-thrift decor at **Café Langereis** (cafelangereis.nl; Amstel 202; ⊘11am-3am Sun-Thu, to 4am Fri & Sat; 🛜; 🚊4/9/14 Rembrandtplein), at the foot of the Blauwbrug (Blue Bridge).

❶ Groenburgwal

Step out onto the white drawbridge that crosses the **Groenburgwal** and look north. Many Amsterdammers swear this is the loveliest canal view of all – a pick backed by Impressionist Claude Monet, who painted it in 1874 as *The Zuiderkerk (South Church) at Amsterdam: Looking up the Groenburgwal.*

❷ NAP Display

Head to the **Stopera** building, Amsterdam's combination of city hall and Muziektheater (p138). Inside check out the **Normaal Amsterdams Peil (NAP) Visitors Centre**. NAP is the Netherlands' sea-level measurement, and exhibits here show how much of Amsterdam falls below it.

❸ Blauwbrug

Cross the river via the 1884 **Blauwbrug** (Blue Bridge). Inspired by Paris' Alexander III bridge, it features tall, ornate street lamps topped by the imperial crown of Amsterdam, fish sculptures, and

View from the Groenburgwal towards Zuiderkirk

DENNIS VAN DE WATER / SHUTTERSTOCK ©

foundations shaped like a medieval ship prow.

④ Reguliersgracht

Walk along the Herengracht to **Reguliersgracht** (p72), the 'seven bridges' canal. Stand with your back to the Thorbeckeplein and the Herengracht flowing directly in front of you. Lean over the bridge and sigh at the seven humpbacked arches leading down the canal straight ahead.

⑤ Magere Brug

Walk along the Keizergracht and turn right toward the wedding-photo-favourite **Magere Brug** (Skinny Bridge). According to legend, two sisters built it. They lived on opposite sides of the river and wanted an easy way to visit each other. Alas, they only had enough money to construct a narrow bridge.

⑥ Amstelsluizen

Continue south to the **Amstelsluizen**. These impressive locks, dating from 1674, allow the canals to be flushed with fresh water. The sluices on the city's west

side are left open as the stagnant water is pumped out to sea.

⑦ De Ysbreeker

Cross the river once more; take Prof Tulpplein past the Inter-Continental hotel to **De Ysbreeker** (p122). The building used to be an inn for the tough guys who broke ice on the Amstel so boats could pass. Grab a seat on the enormous waterfront terrace to see what's gliding by these days.

Best Walks
Cheese, Gin & Monuments

🏃 The Walk

This tour is a hit parade of Amsterdam's favourite foods and historic sights. Swoop through the Western Canals and City Centre, gobbling up traditional *kaas* (cheese), *haring* (herring) and *jenever* (gin) in between stops at the city's birthplace, its Royal Palace and a Golden Age art cache. It's a big bite of Amsterdam in under two hours. The best time to trek is early afternoon, when opening times for the sights and bars coincide.

Start De Kaaskamer, 🚋 1/2/5 Spui

Finish Wynand Fockink, 🚋 4/9/16/24 Dam

Length 2km; 1½ to two hours with stops

🍴 Take a Break

Inviting *cafés* and brainy bookstores ring the Spui (pronounced 'spow'; rhymes with 'now'), a broad square where academics and journalists hang out. **Hoppe** (p35) has poured for the literati for over 340 years.

De Kaaskamer

❶ De Kaaskamer

The Dutch eat more than 14kg of cheese per person annually and it appears much of that hunky goodness is sold right here in **De Kaaskamer** (p62). Wheels of Gouda, Edam and other locally made types stack up to the rafters. Get a wedge to go.

❷ Begijnhof

On the Spui, just past the American Book Center, is a humble wood door. Push it open and behold the hidden community known as the **Begijnhof** (p28) surrounding two historic churches and gardens. Cross the courtyard to the other entrance.

❸ Civic Guard Gallery

From the Begijnhof turn north and walk a short distance to the **Civic Guard Gallery** (p29). Paintings of stern folks in ruffled collars stare down from the walls. Cross the gallery and depart through the Amsterdam Museum's courtyard restaurant onto Kalverstraat.

❹ Royal Palace

Kalverstraat deposits you by the **Royal Palace** (p24), King Willem-Alexander's pad, though he's rarely here, preferring Den Haag for his digs. The sumptuous interior deserves a look.

❺ Nieuwe Kerk

The palace's neighbour is the **Nieuwe Kerk** (p29), the stage for Dutch coronations. Take time to admire the 15th-century architecture.

❻ Rob Wigboldus Vishandel

C'mon, stop being shy about eating raw fish. Try the famed Dutch herring at **Rob Wigboldus Vishandel** (p32), a teeny three-table shop. Once sated, depart Zoutsteeg onto Damrak.

❼ Dam

Cross Damrak so you're on the Nationaal Monument side of the **Dam** (p30) – Amsterdam's birthplace. Wade through the sea of bikes to see the urns behind the monument, which hold earth from East Indies war cemeteries. Now follow the street leading behind the NH Grand Hotel Krasnapolsky.

❽ Wynand Fockink

'Sshh, the *jenever* is resting', says the admonition over the door at **Wynand Fockink** (p34). The Dutch-gin maker's tasting room dates from 1679. The barkeep will pour your drink to the brim, so do like the locals to prevent spillage: lean over it and sip without lifting.

Best
Museums &
Galleries

Amsterdam's world-class museums draw millions of visitors each year. The art collections take pride of place – you can't walk a kilometre without bumping into a masterpiece here. Canal-house museums are another local speciality. And, of course, the freewheeling city has a fine assortment of oddball museums dedicated to everything from handbags to houseboats.

All the Art

The Dutch Masters helped spawn the prolific art collections around town. You've probably heard of a few of these guys: Jan Vermeer, Frans Hals and Rembrandt van Rijn. They came along during the Golden Age when a new, bourgeois society of merchants, artisans and shopkeepers were spending money to brighten up their homes and workplaces. The masters were there to meet the need, and their output from the era now fills Amsterdam's top museums.

Other Treasures

The Netherlands' maritime prowess during the Golden Age also filled the coffers of local institutions. Silver, porcelain and colonial tchotchkes picked up on distant voyages form the basis of collections in the Rijksmuseum, Amsterdam Museum, Het Scheepvaartmuseum and Tropenmuseum.

Canal-House Museums

There are two kinds: the first preserves the house as a living space, with sumptuous interiors that show how the richest locals lived once upon a time, as at Museum Van Loon. The other type uses the elegant structure as a backdrop for unique collections, such as the Kattenkabinet for cat art.

FOTOGRAFIE K J SCHRAA / GETTY IMAGES ©

☑ Top Tips

▶ Take advantage of e-tickets. Most sights sell them and there's little to no surcharge. They typically allow entry via a separate, faster queue.

▶ Queues are shortest during late afternoon and evening.

▶ The I Amsterdam Card (per 24/48/72 hours €49/59/69) can save money; get it at the VVV I Amsterdam Visitor Centre.

Best Art Museums

Van Gogh Museum
Hangs the world's largest collection of the tortured artist's vivid swirls. (p86)

Rijksmuseum The Netherlands' top treasure house bursts with Rembrandts, Vermeers, Delftware and more. (p90; pictured left)

Museum het Rembrandthuis
Immerse yourself in the old master's paint-spattered studio and handsome home. (p126)

Stedelijk Museum Renowned modern art from Picasso to Mondrian to Warhol stuffs the wild-looking building. (p97)

Hermitage Amsterdam
The satellite of Russia's Hermitage Museum features one-off, blockbuster exhibits. (p72)

FOAM Hip photography museum with changing exhibits by world-renowned shutterbugs. (p73)

Best History Museums

Anne Frank Huis The Secret Annexe and Anne's claustrophobic bedroom serve as chilling reminders of WWII. (p44)

Amsterdam Museum
Whiz-bang exhibits take you through the twists and turns of Amsterdam's convoluted history. (p28)

Verzetsmuseum Learn about WWII Dutch resistance fighters during the German occupation. (p132)

Best Offbeat Museums

Kattenkabinet A creaky old canal house filled with kitty-cat art, including a Picasso. (p69)

Tassenmuseum Hendrikje An entire museum devoted to handbags, from 16th-century goatskin pouches to Madonna's modern arm candy. (p73)

Pianola Museum Listen to rare jazz and classical tunes unrolling on vintage player pianos. (p50)

Amsterdam Pipe Museum Chinese opium pipes, Turkish water pipes, ancient Ecuadorian pipes and more cram the cabinets. (p74)

Best Canal-House Museums

Museum Van Loon This opulent old manor whispers family secrets in its shadowy rooms. (p72)

Museum Willet-Holthuysen Sumptuous paintings, china and a French-style garden with sundial. (p72)

Best Underappreciated Museums

Tropenmuseum A whopping collection of ritual masks, spiky spears and other colonial booty. (p120)

Het Scheepvaartmuseum The Maritime Museum features ancient globes, spooky ship figureheads and a replica schooner to climb. (p144)

Museum Ons' Lieve Heer op Solder Looks like an ordinary canal house, but hides a relic-rich 17th-century church inside. (p28)

Best Galleries

Civic Guard Gallery
Check out the collection of enormous portraits, from Golden Age to modern day. (p29)

De Appel Count on having your mind expanded at this hip contemporary-arts centre. (p129)

Best
Parks & Gardens

RACHEL LEWIS / GETTY IMAGES ©

Amsterdam has around 30 parks, so you're never far from a leafy refuge. City planners built in green spaces to provide relief from the densely packed neighbourhoods. They did a heck of a job. Enter the gates of Vondelpark or any of the other meadow-fringed landscapes, and you're hit with a potent shot of pastoral relaxation.

Best for Strolling & Picnicking

Vondelpark Amsterdam's premier green scene is a mash-up of ponds, thickets and winding paths beloved by kissing couples, free-wheeling cyclists and duck-chasing children. (p94; pictured right)

Westerpark Abutting a former gasworks building turned edgy cultural centre, the west side's rambling, reedy wilderness has become a hipster hang-out. (p65)

Sarphatipark De Pijp's lush oasis of rolling lawns, statues and fountains is similar to Vondelpark but without the crowds. (p107)

Oosterpark Political monuments and grey herons dot the sweeping expanse, built for nouveau-riche diamond traders a century ago. (p122)

Best Gardens

Hortus Botanicus When Dutch ships sailed afar in the 1600s, the tropical seeds they brought back were grown in this wonderful garden. (p133)

Begijnhof Push open the unassuming door and *voila* – a hidden courtyard of flowery gardens appears. (p28)

Rijksmuseum Big-name sculpture exhibitions pop up amid rose bushes and hedges in the museum's free, oft-overlooked gardens. (p90)

Museum Willet-Holthuysen A cosy French-style garden with sundial rolls out behind the gorgeous canal house. (p72)

☑ Top Tips

▸ Jan Pieter Heijestraat and Overtoom accommodate several delis and small markets that are handy for composing a picnic for Vondelpark.

▸ Delicious takeaway shops for picnic fixings line Haarlemmerstraat and Haarlemmerdijk leading into Westerpark.

▸ The shop 't Kaasboertje (p111) provides hearty supplies for outdoor meals in Sarphatipark.

Best
Canals

Amsterdammers have always known their Canal Ring, built during the Golden Age, is extraordinary. Unesco made it official in 2010, when it listed the waterways as a World Heritage site. Today the city's canals outnumber those in Venice, and Amsterdam also has three times as many bridges – more than any other city worldwide.

Best Views

Golden Bend Where the Golden Age magnates built their mansions along the regal Herengracht. (p69; pictured right)

Reguliersgracht The tour favourite 'canal of seven bridges', is one of Amsterdam's most photographed vistas. (p72)

Prinsengracht The liveliest of Amsterdam's inner canals, with cafes, shops and houseboats lining the quays. (p53)

Brouwersgracht Among some seriously tough competition Amsterdammers swear this is the city's most beautiful canal. (p53)

Best Canal-Related Museums

Het Grachtenhuis Inventive multimedia displays explain how the Canal Ring and its amazing houses were built. (p50)

Houseboat Museum Discover how *gezellig* (convivial, cosy) houseboat living can be aboard this 1914 sailing barge-turned-museum. (p51)

Best Canal-Side Dining

De Belhamel At the head of the Herengracht, this superb restaurant's tables along the canal are an aphrodisiac. (p54)

Buffet van Odette Simple, creative cooking overlooking the Prinsengracht's crooked canal houses. (p75)

Gebr Hartering Exquisite modern Dutch dishes compete with an impossibly romantic by-the-water location. (p135)

Best Canal-Side Drinking

't Smalle Dock your boat right by the stone terrace of the 18th-century former *jenever* (Dutch gin) distillery. (p56)

Hannekes Boom Local favourite with a gorgeous leafy beer garden on the water. (p147)

De Ysbreeker Hot spot overlooking the houseboat-dotted Amstel. (p122)

Café Binnen Buiten The best canal-side terrace in Amsterdam's buzzy De Pijp neighbourhood. (p107)

Best
Eating

Amsterdam's food scene is woefully underrated. Beyond pancakes and potatoes, Dutch chefs put their spin on all kinds of regional and global dishes using ingredients plucked from local seas and farms. Wherever you go, meals are something to linger over as the candles burn low on the tabletop.

LONELY PLANET / GETTY IMAGES ©

Dutch Specialities

Traditional Dutch cuisine revolves around meat, potatoes and vegetables. Typical dishes include *stamppot* (mashed pot) – potatoes mashed with veggies (usually kale or endive) and served with smoked sausage or strips of pork. *Erwtensoep* is a thick pea soup with smoked sausage and bacon. *Pannenkoeken* translates as 'pancakes', although North Americans will be in for a surprise – the Dutch variety is huge and a little stretchy, served one to a plate and topped with sweet or savoury ingredients.

Indonesian & Surinamese Fare

The Netherlands' former colonies spice up local fare. The most famous Indonesian dish is *rijsttafel* (rice table): a dozen or more tiny dishes such as braised beef, pork satay and ribs served with white rice. Surinamese food features curries prominently. Roti are burrito-like flatbread wraps stuffed with curried meat or veg; they're delicious, filling and cheap.

Snacks

Vlaamse frites are the iconic French fries smothered in mayonnaise or myriad other gooey sauces. *Kroketten* (croquettes) are dough balls, with various fillings, that are crumbed and deep-fried; the variety called *bitterballen* are a popular brown-*café* snack served with mustard.

☑ **Top Tips**

▶ Many restaurants, even top-end places, do not accept credit cards. Or if they do, they levy a 5% surcharge. Always check first.

▶ Phone ahead to make a reservation for eateries in the middle and upper price brackets. Nearly everyone speaks English. Many places also let you book online.

Best Dutch

Ron Gastrobar Star chef Ron Blaauw operates this spot serving Dutch-style tapas. (p98)

Greetje Resurrects Dutch classics, with mouthwatering results. (p135)

Erwtensoep (pea soup)

Distro Dij Ons I lonest-to-goodness classics include *stamppot*. (p54)

Restaurant Elmar Organic Dutch produce is used in stunning flavour combinations. (p111)

Best Indonesian

Dèsa Hugely popular for its *rijsttafel* (rice table) banquets. (p112)

Restaurant Blauw Feted Indonesian fare in contemporary surrounds. (p100)

Best Surinamese

Tokoman Crowds queue for the hot-spiced Surinamese sandwiches. (p135)

Roopram Roti No-frills spot for flaky roti and fiery hot sauce. (p122)

Best Budget

Fat Dog Ultra-gourmet hot dogs by celeb chef Ron Blaauw. (p110)

Butcher Quite possibly the biggest, freshest burgers you'll ever taste, made right in front of you. (p111)

Braai BBQ Bar Street-food-style hot spot barbecuing tangy ribs. (p99)

Best for Foodies

Gartine Slow-food sandwiches and a dazzling high tea hide in the City Centre. (p30)

De Kas Dine in the greenhouse that grew your meal's ingredients. (p120)

Marius The chef whips up a four-course menu from his daily market finds. (p65)

Best Vegetarian

Lavinia Good Food Superb spelt minipizzas, portobello mushroom burgers and salads. (p77)

De Peper The OT301 squat cooks vegan meals for the masses. (p102)

Best Brunch

Bakers & Roasters Banana nutbread French toast and Bloody Marys at Amsterdam's brunch specialist. (p110)

Scandinavian Embassy Goat's milk yoghurt, salmon on Danish rye bread and more dishes from northern lands. (p111)

Best
Drinking &
Nightlife

Despite its wild party-animal reputation, Amsterdam remains a cafe society, where the pursuit of pleasure is more about cosiness and charm than hedonism. Coffee, beer and Dutch gin fill local cups, each a fine companion for whiling away the afternoon on a sunny canal-side terrace.

LONELY PLANET / GETTY IMAGES ©

Brown Cafés

Bruin cafés (brown cafes) are Amsterdam's crowning glory. The true specimen has been in business a while and is named for centuries' worth of smoke stains on the walls. Brown cafes have candle-topped tables, sandy wooden floors and sometimes a house cat that sidles up for a scratch. Most importantly, brown cafes induce a cosy vibe that prompts friends to linger and chat for hours over drinks – the same enchantment the cafes have cast for some 300 years.

Other Places to Drink

Grand cafés are spacious, have comfortable furniture and are, well, just grand. Designer bars are trendy with cool interiors. *Proeflokalen* (tasting houses) were once attached to distilleries. They're great places to try *jenever* (ya-*nay*-ver), aka Dutch gin.

What to Drink

Lager beer is the staple, served cool and topped by a two-finger-thick head of froth – supposedly to trap the flavour. Heineken and Amstel are the most common brands. Brouwerij 't IJ, Troost and De Prael are delicious local brewers. Besides beer, *cafés* always serve wine and coffee. The latter is quite popular: the Netherlands consumes more java per capita than any other European country besides Denmark.

☑ Top Tips

▶ *Café* means pub; a coffeeshop is where one gets marijuana.

▶ *Een bier*, *een pils* or *een vaasje* is a normal-sized glass of beer; *een kleintje pils* is a small glass.

▶ A *koffie* is black; *koffie verkeerd* (coffee 'wrong') is made with milk, similar to a caffe latte.

Best Brown Cafés

't Smalle Amsterdam's most intimate canal-side drinking, with a gorgeous historic interior. (p56)

Hoppe An icon of drinking history beloved by journalists, bums and raconteurs. (p35; pictured above)

Canalside cafés in the De Wallen area

De Sluyswacht Swig in the lock-keeper's quarters across from Rembrandt's house. (p129)

In 't Aepjen Candles burn all day long in the time-warped, 500-year-old house. (p35)

Best Tasting Houses

Wynand Fockink The 1679 tasting house pours glorious *jenevers*. (p34)

In de Olofspoort A crew of regulars has dedicated *jenever* bottles stocked just for them. (p36)

Best Beer

Café Belgique Belgium's best brews flow from the glinting brass taps. (p35)

Brouwerij 't IJ Wonderful independent brewery at the foot of a twirling windmill. (p137)

Brouwerij Troost Watch beer being brewed through glass windows. (p112)

Best Cocktails

Franklin Fab terrace and creative concoctions such as a 'Picnic at Vondel'. (p100)

Door 74 Speakeasy-style bar mixes some of Amsterdam's wildest drinks. (p79)

Best Coffeeshops

Dampkring Hollywood made the hobbit-like decor and Cannabis

Cup–winning product famous. (p36)

La Tertulia Cool Van Gogh murals mark this quiet spot on the Prinsengracht. (p58)

Best Clubs

Air Hot spot with eco-friendly design, awesome sound and radical DJs. (p78)

Van Dyck Bar Dress to impress for an Ibiza-style night out. (p79)

Best Wine

Glouglou All-natural by-the-glass wines. (p112)

Pata Negra Wonderfully rustic Spanish-style bodega. (p78)

Best
Shopping

During the Golden Age, Amsterdam was the world's warehouse, stuffed with riches from the far corners of the earth. The capital's cupboards are still stocked with all kinds of exotica (just look at that Red Light gear!), but the real pleasure here is finding some odd, tiny shop selling something you'd find nowhere else.

Specialities & Souvenirs

Dutch fashion is all about cool, practical designs that don't get caught in bike spokes. Dutch-designed homewares bring a stylish touch to everyday objects. Antiques, art and vintage goodies also rank high on the local list. Popular gifts include tulip bulbs, Gouda cheese and bottles of *jenever* (gin). Blue-and-white Delft pottery is a widely available quality souvenir. And, of course, clogs, bongs and pot-leaf-logoed T-shirts are in great supply.

Department Stores & Chains

The busiest shopping streets are Kalverstraat by the Dam and Leidsestraat, which leads into Leidseplein. Both are lined with department stores, such as Dutch retailers Hema and De Bijenkorf. The Old South's PC Hooftstraat lines up Chanel, Diesel, Gucci and other fancy fashion brands along its length.

Boutiques & Antiques

At the top of the Jordaan, Haarlemmerstraat and Haarlemmerdijk are lined with hip boutiques and food shops. Just to the south, the Negen Straatjes (Nine Streets) offers a satisfying browse among its offbeat, pint-sized shops. Antique and art buffs should head for the Southern Canal Belt's Spiegel Quarter, along Spiegelgracht and Nieuwe Spiegelstraat.

LONELY PLANET / GETTY IMAGES ©

☑ Top Tips

▶ A surprising number of stores do not accept credit cards, so make sure you have cash on hand.

▶ Useful words to know: *kassa* (cashier), *korting* (discount) and *uitverkoop* (clearance sale).

Best Markets

Albert Cuypmarkt
Soak up local colour and snap up exotic goods at Amsterdam's largest market. (p106)

Waterlooplein Flea Market
Piles of curios, used footwear and cheap bicycle parts for bargain hunters. (p129; pictured above)

Clogs in a souvenir store

Noordermarkt It's morning bliss trawling for organic foods and vintage clothes. (p47)

Best Dutch Design

Frozen Fountain The coolest, cleverest home gadgets and decor you'll ever see. (p60)

Droog The famed collective is known for sly, playful, repurposed and reinvented homewares. (p138)

Moooi Gallery Dutch designer Marcel Wanders showcases his and others' extraordinary works. (p61)

Best Souvenirs

Museum Shop at the Museumplein The one-stop shop for all your

Rembrandt, Vermeer and Van Gogh items. (p103)

Condomerie Het Gulden Vlies Kooky condoms and saucy postcards make gifts like no other. (p39)

Best Fashion

Young Designers United Tomorrow's big names jam the racks here. (p81)

Tenue de Nîmes Uber-cool denim wear and local designer fashions. (p62)

SPRMRKT A major player in Amsterdam's fashion scene. (p63)

Best Books

Pied à Terre The world's largest travel bookshop

will make anyone's feet itch. (p103)

Oudemanhuis Book Market Covered alleyway lined with second-hand booksellers. (p40)

American Book Center English-language books of all kinds sprawl across three floors. (p39)

Best Antiques

Antiekcentrum Amsterdam Quirky indoor mall with stalls of timeworn goods. (p46)

Gastronomie Nostalgie Beautiful old china, goblets, candlesticks and other tableware. (p40)

Eduard Kramer Purveyor of antique Dutch tiles. (p83)

Best For Free

While many travellers may bemoan the high cost of Amsterdam's lodging and dining, look on the bright (and cheap) side. Not only is the entire Canal Ring a Unesco World Heritage site (read: free living museum), but every day there is something to do that is fabulous and free.

LINDRIK / GETTY IMAGES ©

Best Free Sights

Civic Guard Gallery
A freebie part of the Amsterdam Museum that displays monumental portraits. (p29)

Begijnhof Explore the 14th-century covert courtyard and its clandestine churches. (p28; pictured right)

Stadsarchief You never know what treasures you'll find in the vaults of the city's archives. (p74)

ARCAM A fascinating look at Amsterdam's architecture – past, present and future. (p145)

Albert Cuypmarkt Amsterdam's biggest market bursts with cheeses, bike locks and socks, as do the city's many other bazaars – all free to browse. (p106)

Best Free Entertainment

Concertgebouw Sharpen your elbows to get in for Wednesday's lunchtime concert, often a public rehearsal for the performance later that evening. (p102)

Muziektheater More classical freebies fill the air during lunch, this time on Tuesdays. (p138)

Bimhuis Jazzy jam sessions hot up the revered venue on Tuesday nights. (p149)

Openluchttheater Vondelpark's outdoor theatre puts on dance and jazz concerts and kids' shows throughout summer. (p102)

North Sea Jazz Club Emerging musicians let loose in free 'Summer Sessions' during the week and late-night shows on Saturdays. (p65)

Top Tip

▶ Free ferries depart behind Centraal Station to NDSM-werf, northern Amsterdam's edgy art community 15 minutes up-harbour, and to the EYE Film Institute, five minutes across the river.

Best Free Tours

Sandeman's New Amsterdam Tours Young guides show you the centre's top sights. (p171)

Gassan Diamonds Don't know your princess from marquise, river from top cape? Get the shiny lowdown here. (p132)

Best
For Kids

KAVALENKAU / SHUTTERSTOCK ©

Never mind the sex and drugs – Amsterdam is a children's paradise. The small scale, the quirky buildings, the lack of car traffic and the canals all combine to make it a wondrous place for little ones. And the Dutch seem to always be dreaming up creative ways to entertain youngsters.

Best Thrills

NEMO Kid-focused, hands-on science labs inside and a terrace with a splashy summer water feature outside. (p144; pictured right)

Het Scheepvaartmuseum Climb aboard the full-scale, 17th-century replica ship and check out the cannons. (p144)

Tropenmuseum Spend the afternoon learning to yodel, sitting in a yurt or travelling via otherworldly exhibits. (p120)

Vondelpark Space-age slides at the western end, playground in the middle, duck ponds throughout. (p94)

Artis Royal Zoo Extrovert monkeys, big cats, shimmying fish and a planetarium provide all the requisite thrills. (p132)

Centrale Bibliotheek Amsterdam Has a whole children's floor with storytimes, reading lounges and books in English. (p144)

Micropia The world's first microbe museum has a wall of poop, a kissing meter and other inventive exhibits. (p132)

Best Kid Cuisine

Pancakes! Even picky eaters will say yes to these giant spongy discs of goodness. (p56)

Het Groot Melkhuis The Vondelpark's fairytale-like cafe sits next to a sandy playground where kids can run free. (p102)

IJsmolen Try unique Dutch ice-cream flavours by De Gooyer windmill. (p137)

Best Kids' Shops

Het Oud-Hollandsch Snoepwinkeltje Stocks jar after jar of Dutch penny sweets. (p61)

Knuffels Cuddly stuffed animals, spinning mobiles, puppets and puzzles will please young ones. (p138)

Tinkerbell A toy-and-more store fronted by a mechanical bear blowing bubbles. (p83)

Best
Entertainment

Amsterdam supports a flourishing arts scene, with loads of big concert halls, theatres, cinemas and other performance venues filled on a regular basis. Music buffs will be in their glory, as there's a fervent subculture for just about every genre, especially jazz, classical and avant-garde beats.

INGOLF POMPE / GETTY IMAGES ©

Jazz & Classical Music

Jazz is extremely popular, from far-out, improvisational stylings to more traditional notes. Little jazz cafes abound, and you could easily see a live combo every night of the week. Amsterdam's classical music scene, with top international orchestras, conductors and soloists crowding the agenda, is the envy of many European cities.

Rock & Dance Music

Amsterdam's dance music scene thrives, with DJs catering to all tastes. Many clubs also host live rock bands. Huge touring names often play small-ish venues such as the Melkweg and Paradiso; it's a real treat to catch one of your favourites here.

Ticket Shops

Last Minute Ticket Shops (www.lastminute ticketshop.nl) sell half-price seats to comedy, dance, theatre and music performances on the day of the gig. Available shows are announced daily at 10am. You can buy online with a credit card (usually only chip cards work), or in person. Last Minute shops are located in the Stadsschouwburg (p69), Centrale Bibliotheek Amsterdam (p144) and VVV I Amsterdam Visitor Centre (p181).

Best Jazz & Blues

North Sea Jazz Club Concerts by respected musicians, and jam sessions too. (p65)

Bimhuis The heart of the Netherlands' jazz scene beats in this mod harbourfront venue. (p149)

Jazz Café Alto Excellent wee club where you're practically onstage with the musicians. (p81)

Best Rock

Melkweg Housed in a former dairy, it's Amsterdam's coolest club-gallery-cinema-concert hall. (p80)

Paradiso One-time church that preaches a gospel of rock. (p80; pictured above)

Muziekgebouw and Bimhuis

OCCII A former squat that gives the night to edgy alternative bands. (p102)

CC Muziekcafé Weekly and monthly themed music nights   from reggae to soul to rock. (p114)

De Nieuwe Anita Rock out by the stage behind the bookcase-concealed door. (p60)

Best Classical & Opera

Muziekgebouw aan 't IJ Stunning high-tech temple of the performing arts. (p148)

Concertgebouw World-renowned concert hall with superb acoustics. (p102)

Conservatorium van Amsterdam See recitals by students at Amsterdam's snazzy conservatory of music. (p149)

Best Comedy & Theatre

Felix Meritis It's more than 225 years old, but this arts centre is all about modern, experimental theatre and music. (p59)

Boom Chicago Laugh-out-loud improv-style comedy in the Jordaan. (p59)

Stadsschouwburg Large-scale plays, operettas and festivals right on Leidseplein. (p69)

Worth a Trip

The gleaming **EYE Film Institute** (📞 589 14 00; www.eyefilm.nl; IJpromenade 1; ⏰ 10am-7pm Sat-Thu, to 9pm Fri) sits across the IJ from Centraal Station. Movies from the 40,000-title archive stream in four theatres. A view-tastic bar-restaurant and free exhibits in the basement add to the hep-cat vibe. Take the 'Buiksloterweg' ferry from behind Centraal Station; it's a free five-minute ride.

Best
Gay & Lesbian

To call Amsterdam a gay capital doesn't express just how welcoming and open the scene is here. After all, this is the city that gave the world *Butt* magazine. It's also the city that claims to have founded the world's first gay and lesbian bar, and hosts one of the world's largest and most flamboyant Pride parades.

Party Zones

Five hubs party hardest. **Warmoesstraat** in the Red Light District hosts the infamous, kink-filled leather and fetish bars. Nearby on the upper end of the **Zeedijk** crowds spill onto laid-back bar terraces (though some long-time favourites have closed recently). In the Southern Canal Ring, the area around **Rembrandtplein** (aka the 'Amstel area') has traditional pubs and brown *cafés*, some with a campy bent. **Leidseplein** has a smattering of high-action clubs along Kerkstraat. And **Reguliersdwarsstraat**, located one street down from the flower market, draws the beautiful crowd at its trendy, fickle hot spots.

't Mandje Amsterdam's oldest gay bar is a trinket-covered beauty. (p36)

Montmartre Legendary bar where Dutch ballads and old top-40 hits tear the roof off. (p79)

Taboo Bar Good-time happy hours, drag shows and 'pin the tail on the sailor' games. (p79)

Saarein The original sisters' bar, democratised for one and all. (p59)

Mr B For all your jaw-dropping leather, fetish and dungeon wear. (p41)

MERTEN SNIJDERS / GETTY IMAGES ©

☑ Top Tips

▶ Gay Amsterdam (www.gayamsterdam. com) lists hotels, shops and clubs, and provides maps.

▶ Located behind the Westerkerk (p50), Pink Point (www.pinkpoint.org) is part information kiosk, part souvenir shop. Pick up gay and lesbian publications, and news about parties, events and social groups.

▶ Amsterdam Gay Pride (www.pride. amsterdam; pictured above) rages in late July/early August.

Best Tours

Best Walking Tours

Sandeman's New Amsterdam Tours (www.newamsterdamtours.com; donations encouraged; 🕙10am, 11.15am & 2.15pm; 🚊4/9/16/24 Dam) Energetic young guides working on a tip-only basis lead a three-hour jaunt past the top sights of the city centre and Red Light District. Meet at the Nationaal Monument on the Dam, regardless of the weather.

Hungry Birds Street Food Tours (📞06 1898 6268; www.hungrybirds.nl; per person €69, 🕙11am Mon-Sat) Guides take you 'off the eaten track' to chow on Dutch and ethnic specialities. Tours visit around 10 eateries and street vendors over four hours. Book in advance; departure location varies.

Best Bicycle Tours

Mike's Bike Tours (📞622 79 70; www.mikesbiketoursamsterdam.com; Kerkstraat 134; city tours per adult/child from €22/19, countryside from €25/18; 🕙office 9am-6pm Mar-Oct, from 10am Nov-Feb; 🚊16/24 Keizersgracht) Offers a range of fantastic tours around town, the harbour and further afield south along the Amstel River, past dairy farms and windmills. Clientele tends to skew younger.

Yellow Bike (📞620 69 40; www.yellowbike.nl; Nieuwezijds Kolk 29; city/countryside tours €27.50/32.50; 🚊1/2/5/13/17 Nieuwezijds Kolk) The original cycling-tour company. Choose from city tours or the longer countryside tour through the pretty Waterland district to the north.

Best Boat Tours

Those Dam Boat Guys (📞06 1885 5219; www.thosedamboatguys.com; per person €20; 🕙1pm, 3pm & 5pm; 🚊13/14/17 Westermarkt) Cheeky small tours (no more than 11 people) on

electric boats. Feel free to bring food, beer and smoking material for the 90-minute jaunt. Departure is from Cafe Wester (Nieuwe Leliestraat 2).

Blue Boat Company (📞679 13 70; www.blueboat.nl; Stadhouderskade 30; 75-minute tour adult/child €16/8.50; 🕙half-hourly 10am-6pm Mar-Oct, hourly Nov-Feb; 🚊1/2/5/7/10 Leidseplein) Blue Boat's 75-minute main tour glides by the top sights. Evening cruises (adult/child €19.50/15.50) are also offered.

Best
Cycling

BURÇIN TUNCER / GETTY IMAGES ©

Bicycles are more common than cars in Amsterdam. Everyone cycles: young, old, clubgoers in high heels, cops on duty, and bankers in suits. Pedalling not only puts you shoulder to shoulder with locals, it puts the whole bloomin' city within easy reach. And it's easy to get rolling, so don't be shy.

Rental shops are everywhere, and hiring a bike is easy (see p176). Vondelpark and the Eastern Islands are convenient destinations for DIY cycling.

Feeling more ambitious? Travel 20 minutes north of the city centre to **Amsterdam-Noord** and the landscape morphs to windmills, cows and wee farming communities – all accessible via an afternoon bicycle ride. Here's how: take your wheels onto the free Buiksloterweg ferry behind Centraal Station, and cross the IJ River. The ride takes about five minutes, and boats depart continuously throughout the day. Then pedal north along the Noord-hollands Kanaal. Within a few kilometres you're in the countryside. Cycling maps are available at the VVV I Amsterdam Visitor Centre (p181) by Centraal Station. Tour companies also cover the area.

☑ **Top Tip**

▶ Most bikes come with two locks: one for the front wheel (attach it to the bike frame), the other for the back. One of the locks also should be attached to a bike rack.

Best Cycling Spots

Vondelpark Leafy urban oasis. (p94; pictured above)

Eastern Islands Cool contemporary architecture. (p148)

Amsterdam-Noord Windmills and bucolic farmland.

Best Bike Rentals & Tours

Mike's Bike Tours Mellow company with incognito bikes. (p171)

Yellow Bike Has been around Amsterdam the longest, offering stellar tours and rentals. (p171)

MacBike Bright red cruisers, groovy themed maps and convenient locations. (p177)

Black Bikes Un-logoed bikes in all shapes and sizes. (p177)

Survival Guide

Survival Guide

Before You Go

When to Go

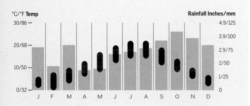

°C/°F Temp
Rainfall Inches/mm

➡ Winter (Dec–Feb)
Ice-skating fun, cosy *cafés* with fireplaces, and low-season rates ease the dark, chilly days.

➡ Spring (Mar–May)
Tulip time! Crowds amass around King's Day (27 April). Alternating rainy and gorgeous weather.

➡ Summer (Jun–Aug)
Peak season, warm with lots of daylight, *café* terraces boom, festivals aplenty.

➡ Autumn (Sep–Nov)
Can be rainy, off-peak rates return, the regular cultural season starts up.

Book Your Stay

☑ **Top Tip** Book as far in advance as possible, especially in summer, and for weekends any time of the year.

➡ Properties often include the 5% city hotel tax in quoted rates, but ask before booking.

➡ If you're paying by credit card, some hotels add a surcharge of up to 5%.

Useful Websites

Lonely Planet (www.lonelyplanet.com/hotels) Find reviews and make bookings.

I Amsterdam (www.iamsterdam.com) Hotels and hostels from the city's official website.

Hotels.nl (www.hotels.nl) For deals on larger properties.

Citymundo (www.citymundo.com) Reliable broker for apartment rentals; three-night minimum.

Best Budget

ClinkNOORD (www.clinkhostels.com) Artsy, avant-garde hostel in artsy, avant-garde Amsterdam-Noord.

Cocomama (www.cocomama.nl) Red-curtained boutique hostel in a former brothel.

Generator Amsterdam (www.generatorhostels.com) Posh new hostel with bars overlooking Oosterpark.

Stayokay Amsterdam Stadsdoelen (www.stayokay.com) Bustling backpacker digs near Nieuwmarkt square.

Best Midrange

Hoxton Amsterdam (www.thehoxton.com) Groovy hipster style at affordable prices.

Collector (www.the-collector.nl) Offbeat B&B in the Old South with backyard chickens.

Hotel Fita (www.fita.nl) Sweet little family-owned hotel a stone's throw from the Museumplein.

Hotel Brouwer (www.hotelbrouwer.nl) Eight artsy rooms in a central, 17th-century canal house.

Best Top End

Sir Albert (www.siralberthotel.com) Diamond factory converted to sparkly design hotel.

Seven One Seven (www.717hotel.nl) Nine spacious, breathtakingly beautiful rooms that you won't want to leave.

Toren (www.thetoren.nl) Blends 17th-century opulence with a sensual decadence.

Hotel Notting Hill (www.hotelnottinghill.nl) A lobby wall of vintage suitcases is among designer Wim Hoopman's touches.

Arriving in Amsterdam

☑ **Top Tip** For the best way to get to your accommodation, see p16.

Schiphol International Airport (AMS)

Train Trains run to Amsterdam's Centraal Station (€5.10 one way, 17 minutes) 24 hours a day. From 6am to 12.30am they go every 10 minutes

Journey Planner

Website 9292 (www.9292.nl) calculates routes, costs and travel times, and will get you from door to door, wherever you're going in the city. The site is in English and Dutch.

or so; hourly in the wee hours. Buy tickets from ticket machines or (usually easier) head past the machines to the ticket windows and purchase from an agent. There's a €0.50 surcharge to use Visa or MasterCard.

Shuttle bus Every 30 minutes from 6am to 9pm, **Connexxion** (www.schipholhotelshuttle.nl; one way/return €17/27) runs a shuttle van from the airport to several hotels. Look for the Connexxion desk by Arrivals 4.

Bus Bus 197 (€5 one way, 25 minutes) is the quickest way to places by the Museumplein, Leidseplein or Vondelpark. It departs outside the arrivals hall door. Buy a ticket from the driver.

Tickets & Passes

➡ The GVB offers handy, unlimited-ride passes for one/two/three days (€7.50/12/16.50), valid on trams, buses and the metro. Longer-duration passes are also available.

➡ Passes are available at the GVB office, I Amsterdam Visitor Centres and from tram conductors (one- and two-day passes only).

➡ The **I Amsterdam Card** (www.iamsterdam.com; per 24/48/72hr €49/59/69) also includes a travel pass.

Taxi Taxis take 20 to 30 minutes to the centre (longer in rush hour), costing around €47. Taxi stand is just outside the arrivals hall door.

Centraal Station (CS)

Tram Ten of Amsterdam's 15 tram lines stop at Centraal Station, and then fan out to the rest of the city, making it simple to reach most lodgings from here. For trams 4, 9, 16, 24 and 26, head far to the left (east) when you come out of the station's main entrance; look for the 'A' sign. For trams 1, 2, 5, 13 and 17, head to the right and look for the 'B' sign.

Taxi Taxis queue near the front entrance toward the west side. Fares are

meter-based. Should be €10 to €15 for destinations in the centre, Canal Ring or Jordaan.

Getting Around

Tram

☑ **Best for...** Most sightseeing and neighbourhood destinations.

➡ Fast, frequent trams operate between 6am and 12.30am.

➡ On trams with conductors, enter at the rear; you can buy a disposable OV-chipkaart (€2.90, good for one hour) or day pass (€7.50) when you board. On trams without

conductors (line 5, and some on line 24), buy a ticket from the driver.

➡ When you enter *and* exit, wave your card at the pink machine to 'check in' and 'check out'.

➡ For further needs, includings maps and pass purchases, visit the **GVB Information Office** (www.gvb.nl; Stationsplein 10; ⊙7am-9pm Mon-Fri, 8am-9pm Sat & Sun; 🚊1/2/4/5/9/14/16/24 Centraal Station). It's across the tram tracks from Centraal Station, and attached to the VVV I Amsterdam Visitor Centre.

Metro & Bus

☑ **Best for...** Some Oosterpark, Nieuwmarkt and Harbour spots.

➡ The metro (subway) and buses primarily serve outer districts. Fares are the same as trams.

➡ *Nachtbussen* (night buses, 1am to 6am, every hour) run after other transport stops. A ticket costs €4.50.

Bicycle

☑ **Best for...** Rolling like a local, Eastern Islands, Vondelpark explorations.

➡ Rental shops are everywhere; most are

open from 9am to 6pm (at least).

→ Prices for single-speed 'coaster-brake' bikes average €11 per 24-hour period. Bikes with gears and handbrakes cost more.

→ Theft insurance costs around €3 extra per day – it's worth getting, as theft is common.

→ You'll have to show a passport or European national ID card, and leave a credit card imprint or pay a deposit (usually €50).

→ **MacBike** (☎620 09 85; www.macbike.nl; Stationsplein 5; bike rental per 3/24hr from €7.50/9.75; ☺9am-5.45pm; ☖4/9/16/24 Centraal Station) is among the most touristy of companies (bikes are bright red, with logos) but has a convenient location at Centraal Station, plus others at Waterlooplein and Leidseplein. Big assortment of bikes available.

→ **Black Bikes** (☎670 85 31; www.black-bikes.com; Nieuwezijds Voorburgwal 146; bike rental per 3/24hr from €6/8.50; ☺8am-8pm Mon-Fri, 9am-7pm Sat & Sun; ☖1/2/5/13/14/17 Dam/

Raadhuisstraat) carry no advertising, so you'll look like a local. The company rents city, kids', tandem and cargo bikes at 10 shops, including this one in the centre.

→ **Mike's Bike Tours** (☎622 79 70; www.mikes biketoursamsterdam.com; Kerkstraat 134; city tours per adult/child from €22/19, countryside from €25/18; ☺office 9am-6pm Mar-Oct, from 10am Nov-Feb; ☖16/24 Keizersgracht) and **Yellow Bike** (☎620 69 40; www. yellowbike.nl; Nieuwezijds Kolk 29; city/countryside tours €27.50/32.50; ☖1/2/5/13/17 Nieuwezijds Kolk) also rent bicycles. Mike's cruisers are signless.

→ Bike locks are usually provided; use them, as theft is rampant.

→ Helmets are generally not available (the Dutch don't wear them).

Boat

☑ **Best for...** North Amsterdam destinations such as EYE Film Institute, NDSM-werf.

→ Free ferries to Amsterdam-Noord depart from piers behind Centraal Station.

→ The ride to Buiksloterweg is the most direct (five minutes) and runs 24 hours.

→ Another boat runs to NDSM-werf (15 minutes) between 7am and midnight (from 9am weekends).

→ Another goes to IJplein (6.30am to midnight).

→ Bicycles are permitted on all routes.

Taxi

☑ **Best for...** Late-night travels; if you have lots of luggage.

→ Find taxis at stands at Centraal Station, Leidseplein and other busy spots around town, or call one; **Taxicentrale Amsterdam** (TCA; ☎777 77 77; www.tcataxi.nl) is the most reliable.

→ Fares are meter-based. The meter starts at €2.95, then it's €2.17 per kilometre thereafter. A ride from Leidseplein to the Dam will cost you about €12.

→ The rideshare company **Uber** (www. uber.com) is popular in Amsterdam. UberX is the legal, low-cost service that operates citywide.

Train

☑ **Best for...** Trips beyond the city.

Amsterdam has convenient train connections with other Netherlands towns and European cities.

➡ For national train schedules (including to/from Schiphol Airport), see NS (www.ns.nl). For international booking and information, see NS International (www.nsinternational.nl).

➡ There are ticket-sales windows in Centraal Station (on the west side) for both national and international destinations.

➡ Note that you'll need cash to buy tickets unless you have a credit card with chip-and-PIN technology.

Car & Motorcycle

➡ Parking is expensive and scarce.

➡ Street parking in the centre costs around €5/30 per hour/day.

➡ It's better (and cheaper) to leave your vehicle in a park-and-ride lot at the edge of town. See www.iamsterdam.com for details.

➡ All the big multinational rental companies are in town; many have offices on Overtoom, near the Vondelpark. Rates start at around €45 per day.

Essential Information

Business Hours

Listings depict operating times for peak season (from around May to September). Opening hours often decrease during off-peak months.

Banks 9am to 4pm Monday to Friday, some Saturday morning.

Cafés, bars & coffeeshops Open noon (exact hours vary); most close 1am Sunday to Thursday, 3am Friday and Saturday.

Clubs Open around 10pm (exact hours vary); close 4am or 5am Friday and Saturday (a few hours earlier on weekdays).

Restaurants Lunch 11am to 2.30pm, dinner 6pm to 10pm.

Shops Large stores: 9am or 10am to 6pm Monday to Saturday, noon to 6pm Sunday. Smaller shops: 10am or noon to 6pm Tuesday to Friday, 10am to 5pm Saturday and Sunday, from noon or 1pm to 5pm or 6pm Monday (if open at all). Many shops stay open late (to 9pm) Thursday.

Discount Cards

The **I Amsterdam Card** (per 24/48/72hr €49/59/69) provides admission to many museums (though not the Rijksmuseum), a canal cruise, and discounts at shops, entertainment venues and restaurants. It also includes a GVB transit pass. Available at VVV I Amsterdam Visitor Centres and some hotels.

Electricity

220V/50Hz

220V/50Hz

Emergency

For police, fire and ambulance, dial 📞 112.

Money

☑ **Top Tip** ATMs are not hard to find, but they often have queues or run out of cash on weekends.

The euro (€) is the currency.

ATMs

➡ Most ATMs accept credit cards such as Visa and MasterCard/Eurocard, as well as cash cards that access the Cirrus and Plus networks.

Credit Cards

➡ Most hotels accept them, but a fair number of shops and restaurants do not, or accept only cards with chip-and-PIN technology (which some American cards lack).

➡ Some businesses levy a 5% surcharge (or more) on credit cards. Always check first.

Money Exchange

➡ Try **GWK Travelex** (Stationsplein; ⏰8am-8pm Mon-Sat, 10am-5pm Sun; 🚃4/9/16/24 Centraal Station) at Centraal Station. There are also branches at Leidseplein and Schiphol Airport.

Tipping

Hotel porters Per bag €1 to €2.

Bars Not expected.

Restaurants For a cafe snack 5% to 10%; for a full meal 10% or so.

Taxis Tip 5% to 10%.

Public Holidays

Banks, schools, offices and most shops close on these days.

Nieuwjaarsdag New Year's Day, 1 January.

Goede Vrijdag Good Friday, March/April.

Eerste & Tweede Paasdag Easter Sunday and Easter Monday, March/April.

Koningsdag King's Day, 27 April.

Bevrijdingsdag Liberation Day, 5 May. This isn't a universal holiday; government workers have the day off, but almost everyone else has to work.

Money-Saving Tips

➡ Make the most of free sights and entertainment – see p166 for tips.

➡ Order the *dagschotel* (dish of the day) or *dagmenu* (set menu of three or more courses) at restaurants.

➡ Check the **Last Minute Ticket Shop** (www.lastminuteticketshop.nl) for half-price, same-day seats for all kinds of performances.

Hemelvaartsdag Ascension Day, 5 May 2016, 25 May 2017.

Eerste & Tweede Pinksterdag Whit Sunday (Pentecost) and Whit Monday, 15/16 May 2016, 4/5 June 2017.

Eerste & Tweede Kerstdag Christmas Day and Boxing Day, 25 and 26 December.

Safe Travel

Amsterdam is generally very safe, but watch your purse or wallet at night in the Red Light District and during the day around the Bloemenmarkt.

Telephone

Mobile Phones

➡ The Netherlands uses GSM phones compatible with the rest of Europe and Australia but not with some North American GMS phones. Smartphones such as iPhones will work – but beware of enormous roaming costs, especially for data.

➡ Prepaid mobile phones are available from around €35. You can also buy SIM cards (from €5) for your own GSM mobile phone that will give you a Dutch telephone number. Look for the Phone House, T-Mobile and Vodafone shops along Kalverstraat and Rokin.

➡ For messaging, a huge percentage of Dutch use WhatsApp (www.whatsapp.com).

Phone Codes

Netherlands country code (📞31)

Amsterdam city code (📞020) Leave off the first 0 when dialling from abroad.

Free calls (📞0800)

Mobile numbers (📞06)

Making International & Domestic Calls

➡ To ring abroad, dial 📞00 followed by the country code for your target country, the area code (you usually drop the leading 0 if there is one) and the subscriber number.

➡ To call locally within Amsterdam, just dial the seven-digit local number (ie do not dial the city code if you are in the area covered by it).

➡ To call a Dutch mobile number locally, dial 06 plus the eight-digit subscriber number.

Toilets

☑ **Top Tip** The standard fee for toilet attendants is €0.50.

➡ Not widespread, apart from the redolent, freestanding public urinals for men in places such as the Red Light District.

Dos & Don'ts

➡ Do give a firm handshake and double or triple cheek kiss.

➡ Don't take photos of women in the red-light windows.

➡ Do dress casually unless it's an overtly formal affair.

➡ Don't smoke dope or drink beer on the streets.

➡ Don't smoke cigarettes inside bars or restaurants.

➡ Many people duck into a *café* or department store.

Tourist Information

➡ The **VVV I Amsterdam Visitor Centre** (Map p26; www.iamsterdam.com; Stationsplein 10; ⊘9am-5pm; 🚊4/9/16/24 Centraal Station), outside Centraal Station, can help with just about anything: it sells the I Amsterdam discount card; theatre and museum tickets; a good city map (€2.50); cycling maps; public transit passes (the GVB transport office is attached); and train tickets to Schiphol Airport. Queues can be long; be sure to take a number when you walk in.

➡ The **VVV I Amsterdam Visitor Centre Schiphol** (⊘7am-10pm), inside the airport at Arrivals 2 hall, offers similar services.

Travellers with Disabilities

➡ Many budget and mid-range hotels have limited accessibility, as they are in old buildings with steep stairs and no lifts.

➡ The city's many cobblestone streets are rough for wheelchairs.

➡ Most buses are wheelchair accessible, as are metro stations.

➡ Trams are becoming more accessible as new equipment is added. Lines 1, 5, 13, 17 and 26 have several elevated stops for wheelchair users.

➡ Accessible Travel Netherlands publishes a downloadable guide (www.accessibletravelnl. com/blogs/New-city-guide-for-Amsterdam) of restaurants, sights, transport and routes in Amsterdam for those with limited mobility.

Visas

➡ Tourists from nearly 60 countries – including Australia, Canada, Israel, Japan, New Zealand, Singapore, South Korea, the USA and most of Europe – need only a valid passport to visit the Netherlands for up to three months.

➡ EU nationals can enter for three months with just their national identity card.

➡ Nationals of most other countries need a Schengen visa, valid within the EU member states (except the UK and Ireland), plus Norway and Iceland, for 90 days within a six-month period.

➡ The Netherlands Foreign Affairs Ministry (www.government.nl) lists consulates and embassies around the world that issue visas.

Language

The pronunciation of Dutch is fairly straightforward. If you read our coloured pronunciation guides as if they were English, you'll be understood just fine. Note that **öy** is pronounced as the 'er y' (without the 'r') in 'her year', and **kh** is a throaty sound, similar to the 'ch' in the Scottish *loch*. The stressed syllables are indicated with italics.

Where relevant, both polite and informal options in Dutch are included, indicated with 'pol' and 'inf' respectively.

To enhance your trip with a phrasebook, visit **lonelyplanet.com**. Lonely Planet iPhone phrasebooks are available through the Apple App store.

Basics

Hello.	*Dag./Hallo.*	dakh/ha·loh
Goodbye.	*Dag.*	dakh
Yes.	*Ja.*	yaa
No.	*Nee.*	ney

Please.
Alstublieft. (pol) al·stew·*bleeft*
Alsjeblieft. (inf) a·shuh·*bleeft*

Thank you.
Dank u/je. (pol/inf) dangk ew/yuh

Excuse me.
Excuseer mij. eks·kew·*zeyr* mey

How are you?
Hoe gaat het met hoo khaat huht met
u/jou? (pol/inf) ew/yaw

Fine. And you?
Goed. En met khoot en met
u/jou? (pol/inf) ew/yaw

Do you speak English?
Spreekt u Engels? spreykt ew *eng*·uhls

I don't understand.
Ik begrijp ik buh·*khreyp*
het niet. huht neet

Eating & Drinking

I'd like ...
Ik wil graag ... ik wil khraakh ...

a beer	*een bier*	uhn beer
a coffee	*een koffie*	uhn ko·fee
a table for two	*een tafel voor twee*	uhn taa·fuhl vohr twey
the menu	*een menu*	uhn me·new

I don't eat (meat).
Ik eet geen (vlees). ik eyt kheyn (vleys)

Delicious!
Heerlijk!/Lekker! heyr·luhk/le·kuhr

Cheers!
Proost! prohst

Please bring the bill.
Mag ik de makh ik duh
rekening rey·kuh·ning
alstublieft? al·stew·*bleeft*

Shopping

I'd like to buy ...
Ik wil graag ... ik wil khraakh ...
kopen. koh·puhn

I'm just looking.
Ik kijk alleen maar. ik keyk a·*leyn* maar

How much is it?
Hoeveel kost het? hoo·*veyl* kost huht

That's too expensive.
Dat is te duur. dat is tuh dewr

Can you lower the price?
Kunt u wat van de kunt ew wat van duh
prijs afdoen? preys *af*·doon

Emergencies

Help!
Help! help

Call a doctor!
Bel een dokter! bel uhn *dok*·tuhr

Call the police!
Bel de politie! bel duh poh·*leet*·see

I'm sick.
Ik ben ziek. ik ben zeek

I'm lost.
Ik ben verdwaald. ik ben vuhr·*dwaalt*

Where are the toilets?
Waar zijn de waar zeyn duh
toiletten? twa *le* tuhn

Time & Numbers

What time is it?
Hoe laat is het? hoo laat is huht

It's (10) o'clock.
Het is (tien) uur. huht is (teen) ewr

Half past (10).
Half (elf). half (elf)
(lit: half eleven)

morning	*'s ochtends*	*sokh*·tuhns
afternoon	*'s middags*	*smi*·dakhs
evening	*'s avonds*	*saa*·vonts
yesterday	*gisteren*	*khis*·tuh·ruhn
today	*vandaag*	van·*daakh*
tomorrow	*morgen*	*mor*·khuhn

1	*één*	eyn
2	*twee*	twey
3	*drie*	dree
4	*vier*	veer
5	*vijf*	veyf
6	*zes*	zes
7	*zeven*	*zey*·vuhn
8	*acht*	akht
9	*negen*	*ney*·khuhn
10	*tien*	teen

Transport & Directions

Where's the ...?
Waar is ...? waar is ...

How far is it?
Hoe ver is het? hoo ver is huht

What's the address?
Wat is het adres? wat is huht a·*dres*

Can you show me (on the map)?
Kunt u het mij kunt ew huht mey
tonen (op de *toh*·nuhn (op duh
kaart)? kaart)

A ticket to ..., please.
Een kaartje naar uhn *kaar*·chuh naar
..., graag. ... khraakh

Please take me to ...
Breng me breng muh
alstublieft al·*stew*·*bleeft*
naar ... naar ...

Does it stop at ...?
Stopt het in ...? stopt huht in ...

I'd like to get off at ...
Ik wil graag in ... ik wil khraak in ...
uitstappen. *öyt*·sta·puhn

Can we get there by bike?
Kunnen we er *ku*·nuhn wuh uhr
met de fiets heen? met duh feets heyn

Behind the Scenes

Send Us Your Feedback

We love to hear from travellers – your comments help make our books better. We read every word, and we guarantee that your feedback goes straight to the authors. Visit **lonelyplanet.com/contact** to submit your updates and suggestions.

Note: We may edit, reproduce and incorporate your comments in Lonely Planet products such as guidebooks, websites and digital products, so let us know if you don't want your comments reproduced or your name acknowledged. For a copy of our privacy policy visit lonelyplanet.com/privacy.

Our Readers

Many thanks to the travellers who used the last edition and wrote to us with helpful hints, advice and anecdotes: Diego Espinoza, Stephen Garone, Umar Akbar

Karla's Thanks

Many thanks to Manon Zondervan, Machteld Ligtvoet and the Amsterdam Press Office, and to Thierry and Julie Lehto, Saskia Maas, Andrew Moskos, Gert-Jan Ruiter and Rachael Teo for sharing their time and excellent info.

Deep gratitude to ace co-author Catherine Le Nevez, Kate Morgan and all at LP. Thanks most of all to Eric Markowitz, the world's best partner-for-life, who accompanied me on the journey and drank loads of beers, visited heaps of museums and carried home all of my Dutch chocolates with the patience of a saint.

Acknowledgments

Cover photograph: Amsterdam, Maurizio Rellini/4Corners
Photograph on pp4–5: Bicycle in Amsterdam, marilynyee/Getty

This Book

This 4th edition of Lonely Planet's *Pocket Amsterdam* guidebook was researched and written by Karla Zimmerman, with content contributions from Catherine Le Nevez. Karla also wrote the previous edition. This guidebook was produced by the following:

Destination Editor Kate Morgan

Product Editors Alison Ridgway, Vicky Smith

Regional Senior Cartographer David Kemp

Book Designer Michael Buick

Assisting Editors Carolyn Bain, Victoria Harrison, Simon Williamson

Cover Research Naomi Parker

Thanks to Neill Coen, Jo Cooke, Brendan Dempsey, Kate Kiely, Kirsten Rawlings, Lauren Wellicome, Tony Wheeler

Index

See also separate subindexes for:

⊗ Eating p188

◔ Drinking p189

✪ Entertainment p189

⌂ Shopping p190

Sights **000**
Map Pages **000**

Sights **000**
Map Pages **000**

Our Writers

Karla Zimmerman

During her Amsterdam travels, Karla admired art, bicycled crash-free, ate an embarrassing quantity of *frites* and bent over to take her *jenever* like a local. She has been visiting Amsterdam since 1989, decades that have seen her trade space cakes for *stroopwafels*, to a much more pleasant effect. She never tires of the city's bobbing houseboats, cling-clinging bike bells and canal houses tilting at impossible angles.

Karla writes travel features for books, magazines and online outlets. She has authored or co-authored several Lonely Planet guidebooks covering the USA, Canada, the Caribbean and Europe. Learn more by following her on Twitter and Instagram (@karlazimmerman).

Contributing Writer

Catherine Le Nevez contributed to the Nieuwmarkt & Plantage, Harbour & Eastern Islands, Southern Canal Belt, Vondelpark & Old South and De Pijp chapters.

Published by Lonely Planet Publications Pty Ltd
ABN 36 005 607 983
4th edition – May 2016
ISBN 9781742208930
© Lonely Planet 2016   Photographs © as indicated 2016
10 9 8 7 6 5 4 3 2 1
Printed in China

Although the authors and Lonely Planet have taken all reasonable care in preparing this book, we make no warranty about the accuracy or completeness of its content and, to the maximum extent permitted, disclaim all liability arising from its use.